Handmade Gifts
FROM THE KITCHEN

More than 100 culinary inspired presents to make and bake

ALISON WALKER

Photography by
Tara Fisher

jacqui
small

COUNTRY LIVING
magazine

First published in 2014 by
Jacqui Small LLP
An imprint of Aurum Press
74–77 White Lion Street
London N1 9PF

Publisher: **Jacqui Small**
Managing Editor: **Lydia Halliday**
Photographer: **Tara Fisher**
Art Director and Designer: **Penny Stock**
Design Concept: **Laura Woussen**
Project Manager and Editor: **Nikki Sims**
Prop Stylist: **Caroline Reeves**
Production: **Maeve Healy**

ISBN 978 1 909342 01 9

A catalogue record for this book is available
from the British Library.

2016 2015 2014
10 9 8 7 6 5 4 3 2 1

Printed in China

When following the recipes, stick to one
set of measurements (metric or imperial).
Measurements used in the recipes are based
on the following conversions:
25g = 1oz
30ml = 1fl oz

Oven temperatures are for conventional
ovens, for fan ovens please reduce the
temperature by 20°C/68°F accordingly.

Contents

INTRODUCTION

I love to cook and spend as much time in my kitchen as possible. But it's not just the act of cooking itself that fills me with joy. The true pleasure comes from sharing food that I've made for family and friends. A sweet or savoury home-made gift, thoughtfully created for someone special will always be more appreciated than any shop-bought version.

Throughout the year, I stock my pantry with seasonal treats, such as jams, chutneys and liqueurs that make wonderful impromptu gifts – and something more interesting to take to a dinner party than a bottle of wine! Any festive occasion is the perfect excuse for me to rustle up cakes, bread or batches of sweets, whether it's Christmas, Easter or Valentine's Day. At Christmas time, I pack gift bags with an assortment of goodies that are handed to guests as they leave.

You'll find all sorts of recipes in this book – from simple things to make with children, such as the tiffin and chocolate mendiants, to savoury biscuits and chutney that can be paired with a favourite cheese to truly impressive and glamorous macarons and truffles displayed in pretty boxes tied with a luxurious ribbon. I haven't forgotten gifts for the cooks themselves, either, with ideas for Italian temptations and a whole gingerbread house to build and decorate among others.

Why make rather than buy? Well, most of the time it's much cheaper than buying something from a shop, it's a good way to use up any garden gluts, you know exactly what has gone into it, it's a pleasure for the cook as well as the recipient and, above all, it's a gift made with love. And what could be better than that?

Alison

Baked
with love

SPICED STARS

PREPARATION: *35 minutes,*
  plus chilling
COOKING: *8 minutes*
MAKES: *about 40*

110g (3¾oz) butter, plus extra
  for greasing
75g (2¾oz) black treacle
seeds from 4 green cardamom
  pods, crushed
¼ tsp freshly ground black
  pepper

50g (1¾oz) caster sugar
1 tbsp ground almonds
200g (7oz) plain flour
½ tsp bicarbonate of soda
½ tsp ground allspice
1 egg yolk, beaten

TO DECORATE (OPTIONAL):
royal icing (about 200g (7oz))
caster sugar, for sprinkling

I think that Scandinavians do spice really well, and these Scandi-style biscuits are flavoured with aromatic cardamom and black pepper. I find the flavour improves with keeping, so it's a good idea to make these the week before giving your gift.

1 Melt the butter and treacle in a pan on a gentle heat. Cool a little.
2 In a large bowl mix all of the dry ingredients together and make a well in the centre. Pour in the treacle mixture followed by the egg yolk. Mix to form a soft dough and then wrap in clingfilm – it will be very soft but don't worry. Chill for at least an hour until the dough is firm but still pliable. Meanwhile, preheat the oven to 190°C/375°F/gas mark 5, and lightly grease two to three baking sheets.
3 Remove the dough from the fridge, divide it into two and roll out each piece on a lightly floured surface to a thickness of 5mm (¼in). Using 7cm (2¾in) and 5cm (2in) star-shaped cutters, stamp out shapes, re-rolling the trimmings as necessary. Arrange on the baking sheets, spacing them apart.
4 Bake in a preheated oven for 6–8 minutes.
5 Remove from the oven and leave to cool for 5 minutes on the baking sheets until set, then transfer to wire racks to cool.
6 If you'd like to decorate your stars, fill a piping bag with royal icing and pipe shapes onto the biscuits. While the icing is still wet, dust lightly with caster sugar, shaking off the excess. Leave to dry completely, before packing in cellophane. These biscuits keep for up to four weeks in an airtight container or sealed packet.

CHERRY AND ALMOND BISCOTTI

PREPARATION: *35 minutes*
COOKING: *1 hour 5 minutes*
MAKES: *about 60*

250g (9oz) 00 Italian flour
¼ tsp baking powder
225g (8oz) golden caster sugar
2 large eggs, beaten with 1 tsp
  almond extract
finely grated zest 1 lemon
100g (3½oz) blanched almonds,
  toasted and roughly chopped
100g (3½oz) dried cherries

I find these moreish Italian biscuits are perfect partners to a glass of Vin Santo or an after-dinner espresso.

1 Preheat the oven to 200°C/400°F/gas mark 6. Lightly grease a large baking sheet; you'll need a couple more later on.

2 Sift the flour onto a work surface with the baking powder, then make a large well in the centre, by pushing the flour to the edge.

3 Put the sugar, eggs and lemon zest in the centre and gradually work in the flour with the fingertips of one hand. (You could do this in a bowl, beating the eggs and sugar together before adding the flour, but the messy method is more fun and actually easier to do.)

4 When the eggs and sugar are thoroughly incorporated, knead in the almonds and cherries.

5 Divide the finished dough into two pieces and shape each into a 'sausage' about 30cm (12in) long and transfer to the baking sheet. Flatten the 'sausage' slightly, so that it's about 3cm (1¼in) high. Bake in a preheated oven for 20 minutes until set and lightly golden.

6 Remove from the oven and cool for a few minutes on a wire rack. Turn down the oven temperature to 150°C/300°F/gas mark 2.

7 Using a serrated knife, slice each biscotti 'sausage' slightly at an angle at 1cm (½in) intervals. Arrange the biscotti in one layer on two or three baking sheets. Bake for 40–45 minutes until dried out.

8 Remove from the oven and cool on wire racks. These crunchy biscotti keep for two months in airtight containers or sealed packets.

CHOCOLATE SHORTBREAD BUTTONS

PREPARATION: *20 minutes,*
 plus chilling
COOKING: *20 minutes*
MAKES: *18–20*

170g (6oz) unsalted butter,
 softened
85g (3oz) caster sugar
1 tsp vanilla extract
150g (5½oz) plain flour, plus
 extra for dusting
85g (3oz) rice flour
20g (¾oz) cocoa powder
a pinch of salt

This is a modern take on the classic shortbread rounds, this time with added chocolate and in a cute button shape; the plain version is equally delicious*. Threading the button holes with twine is a fun touch, too.

1 Preheat the oven to 170°C/325°F/gas mark 3, and line two baking sheets with baking parchment.
2 Cream the butter and sugar together with an electric whisk until soft and fluffy and almost white in colour, then beat in the vanilla extract.
3 Sift together the flours and cocoa powder with the salt, then add to the butter mixture. Blend with a fork to form a dough.
4 Knead on a very lightly floured worktop (be wary of the fact that too much flour will make the biscuits dry) until smooth. Flatten into a disc, wrap in clingfilm and chill for 30 minutes.
5 Take the dough out of the fridge and on a lightly dusted surface roll out to a 5mm (¼in) thickness. Cut out rounds with a plain 6cm (2½in) cutter. Using a 5cm (2in) plain cutter, press just inside the biscuit almost halfway through. With a skewer, make four small holes to represent the holes of a button. Arrange on the baking sheets and chill for 30 minutes.
6 Bake for 10–15 minutes until just firm. If the button markings have blurred during baking, gently re-mark with the cutter and skewer while still warm and pliable. Leave to cool for 1–2 minutes on the trays before transferring to a wire rack to cool. These biscuits keep for four weeks in an airtight container or sealed packet.
* To make the plain shortbread version, simply omit the cocoa powder and use 170g (6oz) of plain flour.

VIENNESE WHIRLS

PREPARATION: *30 minutes*
COOKING: *12 minutes*
MAKES: *15–20*

120g (4oz) unsalted butter, very
   soft, plus extra for greasing
25g (1oz) icing sugar, sifted
120g (4oz) self-raising flour
½ tsp vanilla bean paste

These melt-in-the-mouth biscuits work well in all manner of shapes.
I like this classic whirl, or 'S' shape, but you could make fingers or
flowers simply by piping the mixture into those shapes before you bake
them. Alternatively, transform two biscuits into a Viennese sandwich
with a layer of flavoured buttercream or dip the ends of each biscuit into
melted chocolate. These gifts work equally well as a petit four or served
with a bowl of ice cream; it would be a good idea to put that on the label.

1 Preheat the oven to 190°C/375°F/gas mark 5. Lightly grease one or
two large baking sheets.
2 Beat the butter and icing sugar with an electric whisk until light and
fluffy and almost white in colour. Beat in the vanilla bean paste.
3 Using a fork, blend the flour and baking powder into the butter in
three batches, until smooth.
4 Fit a piping bag with a 1½cm (¾in) star nozzle and fill with the
biscuit mixture. Pipe 'S' shapes on to the baking sheets about 6–7cm
(2½–2¾in) long and space them well apart. (If the mixture becomes
over-soft while piping, chill the bag for a few minutes before resuming.)
5 Bake in a preheated oven for 10–12 minutes until lightly golden at the
edges. Remove from the oven and transfer to a wire rack to cool. These
biscuits keep for four weeks in an airtight container or sealed packet.

LAVENDER MADELEINES

PREPARATION: *25 minutes,*
  plus standing
COOKING: *10 minutes*
MAKES: *18*

100g (3½oz) lavender sugar*
2 medium eggs
100g (3½oz) plain flour, plus
  extra for dusting
¾ tsp baking powder
100g (3½oz) butter, melted, plus
  extra for greasing

These buttery French cakes are instantly recognisable by their pretty scalloped shell shape. Dust with icing sugar or give with some chocolate fudge sauce (see page 111) for dipping them into.

1 Preheat the oven to 200°C/400°F/gas mark 6. Brush a Madeleine tin with melted butter and a good dusting of flour. Tap out the excess.
2 Beat the sugar and eggs until light and fluffy. Fold in the flour and baking powder, followed by the butter. Leave to stand for 30 minutes.
3 Fill each mould three-quarters full of the mixture and bake in a preheated oven for 8–10 minutes until golden and risen. Remove from the oven, leave to cool for a few minutes and transfer to a wire rack.
4 These cakes keep for two to three days in an airtight container or sealed packet but are best eaten on the day they're made.
(* To make lavender sugar, put a handful of lavender flower sprigs into a container of caster sugar. Seal and leave for at least two weeks to infuse before using.)

EARL GREY HEARTS

PREPARATION: *35 minutes,*
  plus chilling
COOKING: *10 minutes*
MAKES: *25–30*

175g (6¼oz) plain flour
50g (1¾oz) icing sugar
1 tsp Earl Grey tea
100g (3½oz) butter, softened, plus
  extra for greasing
1 medium egg yolk

A gently flavoured biscuit that could be gifted to tea lovers with
a packet of their favourite brew.

1 Put the flour, icing sugar and tea into a food processor. Add the rest of
the ingredients and whizz to form a soft dough. Shape into a disc, wrap
in clingfilm and chill for 20 minutes.
2 Meanwhile, preheat the oven to 190°C/375°F/gas mark 5, and lightly
grease two to three baking sheets.
3 Remove the dough from the fridge and lightly flour a work surface.
Roll out to a 5mm (¼in) thickness, cut out shapes with a 5cm (2in) heart-
shaped cutter and space apart on the baking sheets.
4 Bake in a preheated oven for 8–10 minutes until lightly golden. Leave
to cool on the sheets for a couple of minutes before transferring to wire
racks to cool completely. These biscuits keep for up to four weeks in an
airtight container or sealed packet.

STOLLEN WREATH

PREPARATION: 45 minutes,
  plus macerating and rising
COOKING: 40 minutes
SERVES: 10–12

100g (3½oz) each of raisins and
  sultanas
2 tbsp rum
20g (¾oz) dried yeast (or 40g
  (1½oz) fresh yeast)
100ml (3½fl oz) tepid milk
350g (12oz) strong white flour
¼ tsp ground coriander
a grating of fresh nutmeg
50g (1¾oz) caster sugar
1 tsp salt
120g (4oz) soft butter, diced
1 medium egg
sunflower oil, for greasing
50g (1¾oz) candied peel
25g (1oz) blanched almonds,
  split lengthways
finely grated zest of 1 lemon
75g (2¾oz) unsalted butter,
  melted
icing sugar, for dusting

Stollen is traditionally shaped into a flat loaf but here I've opted for a wreath – it would make a stunning centrepiece for a Christmas table.

1 Put the dried fruit into a non-metallic bowl with the rum. Leave to stand overnight.

2 Mix together the yeast and milk, then stir in 100g (3½oz) of the flour. Cover and leave to stand for 2 hours – the mixture should bubble.

3 Mix together the remaining flour with the spices, sugar and salt. Make a well in the centre and add the butter, egg and the yeast mixture. Bring together with your hands – don't worry, it will seem crumbly to start with but that will change once you start kneading.

4 Turn out onto a work surface and knead until smooth and elastic – as the butter is worked into the dough it will become smoother. (Alternatively, use the dough hook attachment on a free-standing mixer and mix for 2 minutes at the lowest speed then 5–7 minutes on medium speed until the dough is nice and elastic.) Turn into a lightly oiled bowl, cover with clingfilm and leave to rise for 2 hours until doubled in size.

5 Turn out the dough onto a lightly floured work surface and press out flat into a rectangle 40cm x 28cm (15¾in x 11in). Sprinkle with the soaked dried fruit, candied peel, almonds and lemon zest. From one long end, roll up the dough into a Swiss roll shape. Cut in half lengthways, carefully turn the cut sides uppermost, then plait like a rope. Transfer to a greased baking sheet and shape into a ring, twisting the two ends together and tucking underneath to hide the join. Cover loosely with oiled clingfilm and leave to prove for 1 hour until doubled in size.

6 Preheat the oven to 180°C/350°F/gas mark 4. Bake for 35–40 minutes; when it's ready, the bottom should sound hollow when tapped. Remove from the oven and cool on a wire rack for 20 minutes, then brush the top and sides with the melted butter, allowing each coat to dry for a few seconds before adding the next.

7 Just before serving or wrapping, dust heavily with icing sugar. This sweet bread keeps for up to a week in an airtight container.

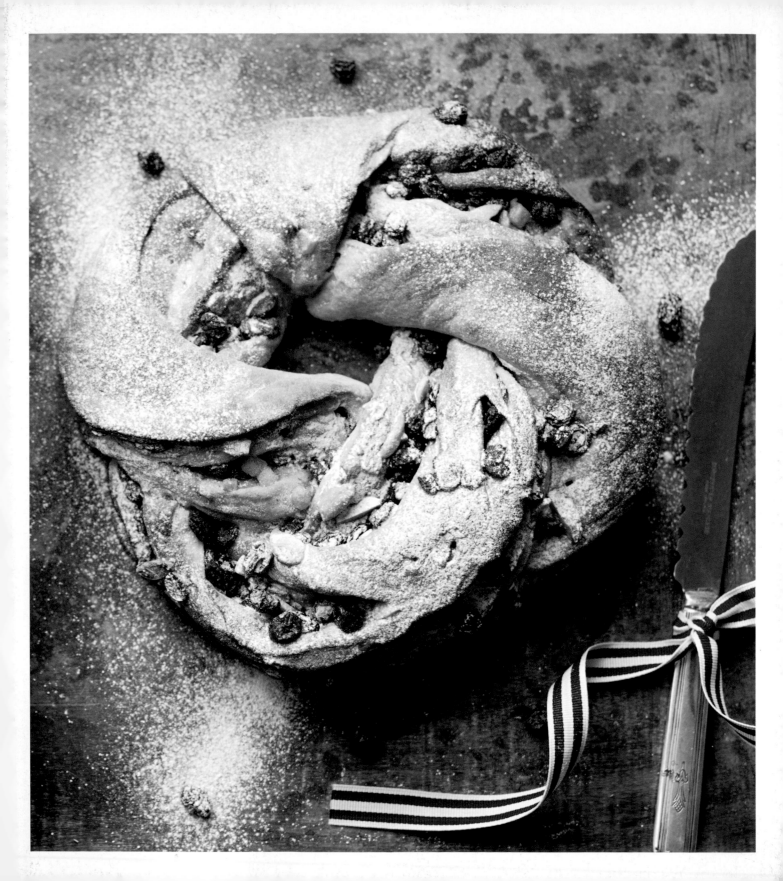

FONDANT CUPCAKES

PREPARATION: *40 minutes*
COOKING: *15 minutes*
MAKES: *18*

FOR THE CUPCAKES:
200g (7oz) golden caster sugar
200g (7oz) unsalted butter, very
*   soft*
finely grated zest and juice of
*   1 lemon*
1–2 tbsp tepid water
4 medium eggs, beaten
200g (7oz) self-raising flour

FOR THE ICING:
600g (1lb 5oz) fondant icing
*   sugar, sifted*
2 tbsp lemon juice
crystallised flowers, to decorate
*   (see right)*

These adorable cupcakes can be adapted to suit any occasion. Tint the icing palest pink for Valentine's Day and decorate with rose petals or embellish with primroses for Mothering Sunday.

1 Preheat the oven to 200°C/400°F/gas mark 6. Line two 12-hole muffin tins with 18 paper cases.
2 Put the cupcake ingredients into a large bowl and beat with an electric whisk for 2 minutes until fluffy and paler in colour.
3 Divide the mixture equally between the paper cases and bake in a preheated oven for 12–15 minutes until golden. Remove from the oven and transfer to a wire rack to cool. The cakes should have fairly flat tops that rise to just below the top of the cake case, but trim if necessary before pouring in the icing.
4 To make the icing, put the icing sugar in a large bowl. Gradually beat in the lemon juice and the water, as necessary, until you have a soft but spreadable consistency that holds its shape.
5 When the cakes are completely cold, flood the icing on top of the cakes up to the edges of the paper cases. Leave to set without moving. When almost set and still slightly wet, decorate with a selection of crystallised flowers (see below).

MAKE YOUR OWN CRYSTALLISED FLOWERS
You can crystallise a variety of flowers and herbs as long as they are edible. My favourites are rose buds and petals, violets, primroses, lavender, mint, rosemary and sweet geranium leaves. Make sure they are unsprayed.
To make crystallised flowers, lightly beat one large egg white until lightly frothy. Using a small paint brush, coat the petals or bud with a little of the egg white. Allow to dry for a few seconds, then sprinkle with caster sugar – this is important because the sugar will become wet and sticky if sprinkled on too quickly. Set on baking parchment to dry – ideally in an airing cupboard or somewhere warm. The flowers will keep in an airtight container for up to a week in a cool, dry place.

MACARONS

PREPARATION: *1 hour, plus resting*
COOKING: *15 minutes*
MAKES: *20*

100g (3½oz) egg whites
100g (3½oz) ground almonds
180g (6½oz) icing sugar
40g (1½oz) caster sugar
¼ tsp vanilla extract
yellow food colouring paste
85g (3oz) good-quality shop-bought lemon curd

1 The day before you make the macarons, separate the eggs and put the whites in a bowl in the fridge loosely covered.

2 When you are ready to make the macarons, bring the egg whites to room temperature. Draw 4cm (1½in) circles at spaced intervals on two to three sheets of baking parchment as a template to guide your piping. Turn it over and use this parchment to line two to three baking sheets.

3 Put the almonds and icing sugar in a food processor and whizz until they become a fine powder. Sieve three times to remove any lumps of almond – this is essential to ensure a smooth surface to your macarons.

4 Whisk the egg whites to a medium peak, then whisk in the caster sugar. Next, whisk in the vanilla extract and food colouring – be generous with the colouring paste as it fades during baking.

5 Using a spatula, fold the almond mixture into the egg whites in two batches – it should be a fairly fluid mix but still be able to be piped.

6 Dot blobs of this mixture on to the underside of each corner of parchment to keep it still during cooking. Transfer the mixture to a piping bag fitted with a large plain nozzle and pipe mounds of the mixture just within the circles. Tap each tray on the work surface a couple of times to remove any air bubbles and leave to stand for anything from 30 minutes to 4 hours (depending on humidity) until the surface of the macarons is no longer tacky – again this is crucial to ensure the macarons have their characteristic frilled feet.

7 Meanwhile, preheat the oven to 160°C/310°F/gas mark 2½. Bake the macarons in a preheated oven for 10–15 minutes until they just peel away from the paper when tested. Remove from the oven and immediately slide the baking parchment with the macarons onto a damp work surface – this will stop them cooking further and also make them easier to remove.

8 Sandwich two shells together with a blob of lemon curd. These macarons keep for up to a week in the fridge. The unfilled shells can be frozen for up to a month.

These elegant treats are sure to elicit 'oohs' and 'aaahs' on their arrival in a box or on a platter. Do make them when you have no other time pressure – they're not difficult to make but they do need to sit for a while ahead of baking to give them that slightly chewy outside. And don't make them on a rainy day, as they never work!

BAKLAVA

PREPARATION: *35 minutes,*
  plus cooling
COOKING: *1 hour 40 minutes*
MAKES: *about 60 pieces*

500g (1lb 2oz) walnuts
60g (2oz) caster sugar
¼ tsp ground cinnamon
a pinch of ground cloves
250g (9oz) ready-made filo pastry
120g (4oz) butter, melted

FOR THE SYRUP:
275g (9¾oz) caster sugar
150ml (5fl oz) water
1 whole clove
finely grated zest of 1 lemon
  (I use unwaxed lemons)
2 tbsp clear honey

This intensely sweet pastry is so versatile – I've made it with hazelnuts and pistachios instead of the walnuts or flavoured the syrup with rosewater or orange-flower water, all with outstanding results.

1 Preheat the oven to 170°C/325°F/gas mark 3. Toast the walnuts in a preheated oven for 5–10 minutes until golden. Tip onto a plate to cool.
2 Coarsely grind the cooled walnuts in a food processor. Tip into a bowl and stir in the sugar and the spices.
3 Cut the filo sheets to the same size as a 30cm x 23cm (12in x 9in) traybake tin and cover with a damp tea towel while you're working to stop them drying out.
4 Brush the base and sides of the tin with melted butter. Lay a filo sheet in the base, brush with butter and lay another sheet on top. Repeat with 8 more sheets, brushing in between with butter as you go.
5 Next, spread with one-third of the walnut mixture. Lay another two filo sheets on top, buttering as before. Repeat this twice more with the remaining walnut mixture.
6 Lay another six sheets of filo on top, again brushing each sheet with butter. Brush the top sheet with butter and mark into diamond shapes. Bake for 1½ hours until golden.
7 Meanwhile, make the syrup. Dissolve the sugar in the water with the clove and lemon zest. Bring to the boil then simmer rapidly for 10 minutes until lightly syrupy. Strain and stir in the honey.
8 Remove the baklava from the oven and immediately pour over half of the syrup. Leave for 30 minutes then slowly pour over the remainder. Leave overnight to infuse but do not chill.
9 Cut the baklava into diamond shapes using the previous markings as a guide. This sticky pastry keeps for up to two weeks in an airtight container or sealed packet.

BILLIONAIRE'S SHORTBREAD

PREPARATION: *35 minutes,*
plus setting
COOKING: *40 minutes*
MAKES: *about 25 pieces*

FOR THE SHORTBREAD BASE:
120g (4oz) plain flour, sifted
60g (2oz) rice flour
60g (2oz) caster sugar
120g (4oz) unsalted butter, diced,
plus extra for greasing

FOR THE SALTED CARAMEL:
397g (14oz) canned sweetened
condensed milk
150g (5½oz) soft dark brown
sugar
150g (5½oz) unsalted butter
½ tsp fine sea salt

FOR THE TOPPING:
100g (3½oz) dark chocolate,
broken into pieces
100g (3½oz) milk chocolate,
broken into pieces
gold powder, for dusting

1 Preheat the oven to 180°C/350°F/gas mark 4, and lightly grease a 30cm x 18cm (12in x 7in) traybake tin.
2 Sift the flours into a large bowl and stir in the sugar. Rub in the butter until the mixture is crumbly and the fat is evenly distributed.
3 Press the shortbread mixture into the base of the prepared tin. Bake for 20–30 minutes until it feels firm to the touch and looks lightly golden. Remove from the oven and set aside in the tin on a wire rack to cool.
4 To make the caramel topping, put the condensed milk, sugar and butter into a heavy-based pan and melt over a low heat to dissolve the sugar. Bring to a gentle boil for about 5 minutes until thickened. Stir in the salt. Pour over the shortbread base and leave in a cool place to set.
5 Put the chocolate in separate heatproof bowls and set over pans of gently simmering water to melt. Stir once or twice until smooth. Pour random pools of the dark chocolate onto the caramel. Fill any gaps with the melted milk chocolate. Using the end of a skewer, swirl the chocolates together to make a pattern. Leave to set at room temperature. Dust with gold powder using a small paintbrush.
6 Cut the biscuits into bite-sized squares. This delightful shortbread keeps for up to a week in an airtight container.

I've ramped up the classic millionaire's shortbread to the next level here and added a luxurious dusting of gold powder.

WEDDING COOKIES

PREPARATION: *30 minutes,*
  plus chilling
COOKING: *15 minutes*
MAKES: *25–30*

60g (2oz) toasted mixed nuts
260g (9¼oz) plain flour
225g (8oz) unsalted butter, very
  soft
30g (1¼oz) icing sugar
½ tsp anise flavouring
¼ tsp salt
icing sugar, for dusting

1 Put the nuts in a food processor with 2 tablespoons of flour and whizz until finely ground – don't overprocess or they will become oily.

2 In a separate bowl, beat together the butter and icing sugar with electric beaters until light and fluffy. Beat in the anise flavouring.

3 Next, beat in the remaining flour and salt until just combined, followed by the blitzed nuts. Chill for 30 minutes or so until firm.

4 Preheat the oven to 180°C/350°F/gas mark 4, and line two baking sheets with baking parchment.

5 Roll pieces of the dough into walnut-sized balls, flatten slightly and arrange on the baking sheets 5cm (2in) apart.

6 Bake in a preheated oven for 12–15 minutes until lightly golden.

7 Remove from the oven and cool on a wire rack. Dredge with sifted icing sugar and package in cellophane or in boxes.

Looking like miniature snowballs, these delightful cookies were once part of tea-sharing ceremonies in Russia during the 18th century and are now often given out as part of wedding celebrations.

Edible flowers are things of beauty in their own right, so I love to use their subtle tastes to enhance the flavour of baking as well as adding to the aesthetics of the finished result. These cookies are real stunners.

ROSE PETAL COOKIES

PREPARATION: *35 minutes,*
  plus chilling
COOKING: *10 minutes*
MAKES: 40–50

120g (4oz) icing sugar, sifted
250g (9oz) plain flour, sifted
250g (9oz) cold butter, diced
2 tbsp unsprayed red rose
  petals, cut into small pieces
  (I use scissors) with white
  heels removed
finely grated zest of 1 lemon

1 Put the sugar, flour and butter into the bowl of a food processor. Whizz until the mixture resembles fine breadcrumbs, then pulse in the rose petals and lemon zest and transfer to a large bowl.
2 Bring it together with your fingers, then lightly knead until smooth.
3 Preheat the oven to 170°C/325°F/gas mark 3, and line two baking sheets with baking parchment.
4 Take walnut-sized pieces of the cookie dough and roll into balls between your palms. Put the dough balls on the baking sheets and press down lightly with a fork to flatten them. Bake in a preheated oven for 10–12 minutes until lightly golden and set.
5 Remove from the oven and leave to cool for a couple of minutes on the baking sheets, then transfer to wire racks to cool. These cookies keep for up to a month in an airtight container or sealed packet.

sweets for
my sweet

HOKEY POKEY

PREPARATION: *25 minutes,*
  plus setting
COOKING: *10 minutes*
MAKES: *350g (12oz)*

100g (3½oz) golden syrup
200g (7oz) golden granulated
  sugar
40g (1½oz) unsalted butter,
  plus extra for greasing
2 tbsp water
2 tsp bicarbonate of soda
½ tsp white wine vinegar
melted chocolate, for dipping
  (optional)

This recipe brings out the child in me: I still love watching the mixture fizz and bubble – volcano-like – as the bicarbonate of soda reacts with the hot sugar syrup to make this wonderful honeycomb.

1 Grease a 16cm x 28cm (6¼in x 11in) traybake tin. Make sure you can leave it somewhere undisturbed as you don't want to move it until the hokey pokey is set.

2 Heat the syrup, sugar and butter in a deep, heavy-bottomed pan until the sugar is dissolved. Using a wet pastry brush, wash down the sides of the pan to dissolve any stray sugar crystals that may cause the sugar syrup to crystallise while cooking.

3 Bring the sugar mixture to the boil and boil steadily until a sugar thermometer reads 138°C/280°F (the soft crack stage). Alternatively, drop a teaspoon of the mixture into a bowl of cold water. Bring it together with your fingers – it should form firm but pliable threads.

4 Take off the heat and immediately stir in the bicarbonate of soda followed by the vinegar – it will fizz and bubble up, so take care.

5 Quickly turn into the prepared tin, pouring in one layer from the top to the bottom of the tin – don't be tempted to smooth out with a spoon or shake the pan to level the mixture because this will burst all the precious bubbles you have just created. Leave to set without moving.

6 Break into pieces and dip into melted chocolate, if you like. These treats start to get sticky after a couple of days but will keep for up to two weeks if completely covered in chocolate.

POPCORN BARK

PREPARATION: *30 minutes*
COOKING: *15 minutes*
MAKES: *36 pieces*

1 tbsp sunflower oil, plus extra
  for greasing
100g (3½oz) popping corn
100g (3½oz) desiccated coconut
100g (3½oz) mini
  marshmallows
175g (6¼oz) golden syrup
200g (7oz) granulated sugar
40g (1½oz) unsalted butter

For some reason, this sticky, chewy treat tastes especially good around an autumn bonfire – maybe it's something to do with the marshmallows combined with the smells in the air...

1 First, cook the popping corn in batches. Heat half the oil in a deep pan over a medium heat. Add half the popcorn kernels, cover with a tight-fitting lid and cook until the kernels start popping. Turn off the heat but leave the pan on the hob and shake occasionally until the kernels stop popping. Pour into a large bowl and set aside to cool. Repeat with the remaining oil and popping corn.

2 When the popcorn has cooled, stir in the coconut and marshmallows. Lightly oil a 23cm x 33cm (9in x 13in) traybake tin.

3 In a heavy-bottomed pan, melt the golden syrup, sugar and butter over a gentle heat until the sugar has dissolved. Using a wet pastry brush, wash down the sides of the pan to dissolve stray sugar crystals that may cause the syrup to crystallise while cooking.

4 Turn up the heat to a steady boil and cook for 4–5 minutes until a sugar thermometer measures 121°C/250°F (the firm ball stage). If you don't have a thermometer, drop a teaspoon of mixture into a bowl of cold water. It should form a firm ball between your fingers.

5 Quickly stir the syrup into the popcorn mixture and immediately turn out into the traybake tin – some of the marshmallows will melt and some will stay whole. Level the mixture and leave to set.

6 Turn out the entire bark onto a board lined with baking parchment. Then use a sharp knife to cut the popcorn bark into squares. This bark keeps for up to a week in an airtight container or sealed packet.

MARZIPAN ALLSORTS

PREPARATION: *55 minutes*
COOKING: *15 minutes*
MAKES: *30–35*

450g (1lb) preserving sugar
150ml (5fl oz) water
¼ tsp cream of tartar
350g (12oz) ground almonds
2 medium egg whites, lightly
  beaten

TO FINISH:
food colouring pastes
icing sugar, for dusting
lightly whisked egg white

A twist on the multilayered liquorice allsort, these sweeties give you a fantastic excuse to play around and create all sorts of multicoloured delights. Once you've mastered making your own marzipan, you can use it to model shapes and cover a mini Christmas cake (see page 142).

1 Put the sugar in a large heavy-bottomed pan with the water. Heat gently to dissolve the sugar then bring to the boil. Add the cream of tartar and boil steadily without stirring until a sugar thermometer reaches 116°C/241°F (the soft ball stage). If you don't have a thermometer, drop a teaspoon of the mixture into a bowl of cold water. Bring it together with your fingers – it should form a soft ball.
2 Take the pan straight off the heat and dip the base in cold water and stir the syrup rapidly until the syrup starts to crystallise or cloud. Stir in the almonds and egg whites and cook for about 3 minutes over a low heat, stirring continuously.
3 Divide this marzipan mixture equally between three bowls and add your chosen colours with a cocktail stick, stirring them in vigorously with a wooden spoon. Be brave with the amount of food colouring as you want them to look vibrant and eye catching.
4 Spread the marzipan out onto plates or a marble slab until cool enough to handle. Dust a surface with icing sugar and knead the marzipan until smooth and pliable; and to make the colour more even. Wrap each portion in baking parchment and leave until cold.
5 Roll each piece into a rectangle roughly 21cm x 15cm (8in x 6in). Brush the top of the first sheet with the egg white and carefully lay the next on top. Smooth over gently with the flat of your hands to remove any air bubbles or bumps. Repeat with another coating of egg white and the final layer of coloured marzipan.
6 Trim away the uneven edges of the marzipan stack using a serrated knife – you will have to clean it regularly as the paste is quite sticky. Cut the layers lengthwise into equal-sized strips then slice crossways into pieces. Arrange the sweets on a large piece of baking parchment and leave to dry until no longer tacky. These allsorts keep for up to three weeks in an airtight container or sealed packet.

PEPPERMINT CANDY CANES

PREPARATION: **50 minutes,**
 plus drying
MAKES: **16**

450g (1lb) icing sugar, sifted
1 tsp lemon juice
1 large egg white, lightly whisked
½ tsp peppermint extract
red food colouring paste

Feeling all retro? These minty canes will transport you back to Christmases past. Whether you make them as jolly decorations for a Christmas tree or as a little extra-something to tie on presents, their arrival always elicits gasps and squeals from children, both big and small.

1 Mix the sugar with the lemon juice and enough egg white to make a stiff paste. Flavour with the peppermint extract.
2 Divide the paste into two pieces. Using a cocktail stick, smear a little red colouring onto one piece, then knead well until the dough is a uniform colour.
3 Make walnut-sized balls from both pieces of paste. Roll each ball into a sausage shape and then twist a white and red 'sausage' together. Roll lightly so that they stick together and smooth the joins. Cut in half.
4 Bend into a cane shape, trim if necessary and leave to dry completely on a piece of baking parchment. These sweeties keep for four weeks in an airtight container or sealed packet.

COCONUT ICE

PREPARATION: *25 minutes*
COOKING: *10 minutes*
MAKES: *24 pieces*

sunflower oil, for greasing
900g (2lb) granulated sugar
300ml (10fl oz) whole milk
300g (10½oz) desiccated coconut
pink food colouring paste

Cut into whatever sized pieces suit your container or wrap in cellophane and tie with ribbon or butcher's twine.

Many adults will disappear into a moment of nostalgia when greeted with this pink-and-white sweet treat; it's one of the first sweets I made as a child, along with peppermint creams. A word of warning about food colouring, though; do be careful when adding the pink colour – a dab too far and a pleasant pastel pink can become intensely lurid.

1 Lightly oil a 16cm x 20cm (6¼in x 7¾in) cake tin, and fill the sink or a large basin with cold water.

2 To make the bottom layer, put half the sugar and half the milk into a heavy-bottomed pan and heat gently until the sugar has dissolved. Using a wet pastry brush, wash down the sides of the pan to dissolve any stray sugar crystals that may cause the sugar syrup to crystallise while cooking.

3 Bring the sugar mixture to the boil and boil steadily until a sugar thermometer reads 116°C/241°F (the soft ball stage). If you don't have a thermometer, drop a teaspoon of the mixture into a bowl of cold water. It should form a soft ball between your fingers.

4 Plunge the base of the pan into the sink or basin of cold water to stop the syrup cooking.

5 Quickly stir in half the coconut and turn into the prepared tin.

6 Repeat step 2 with the remaining sugar and milk. Continue as before and then stir in the remaining coconut with a dab of pink food colouring until evenly pink and pour over the white layer.

7 While it's still soft, mark into bars or squares with a knife. When the coconut ice is completely cold, cut it into the bars. This sweet treat keeps for up to a month in an airtight container or sealed packet so can be made well in advance of giving.

TURKISH DELIGHT

PREPARATION: *20 minutes,*
plus setting
COOKING: *45 minutes*
MAKES: *36 pieces*

sunflower oil, for greasing
500g (1lb 2oz) granulated sugar
1 tbsp liquid glucose
75g (2¾oz) cornflour
200g (7oz) icing sugar
1 litre (1¾ pints) water
60g (2oz) clear honey
1 tsp of flavouring (rosewater,
lemon extract, peppermint
extract or orange-flower water)
a dab of pink, yellow or green
food colouring paste
cornflour and icing sugar, for
dredging

For some reason, I always think of Turkish delight as an exotic, grown-up treat – probably a combination of the 'glamorous' advert that was televised when I was growing up and the fact that my mother always kept it tucked out of reach on a high shelf.

1 Grease an 18cm (7in) square tin (or one of similar dimensions). Fill the sink or a large bowl with cold water.
2 Put the sugar and liquid glucose in a large heavy-bottomed pan with 150ml (5fl oz) of the water. Gently heat until the sugar has dissolved. Wash down the sides of the pan with a pastry brush dipped in water to dissolve any sugar crystals.
3 Bring the sugar mixture to the boil and boil steadily until a sugar thermometer reads 116°C/241°F (the soft ball stage). If you don't have a thermometer, drop a teaspoon of the mixture into a bowl of cold water. Bring it together with your fingers – it should form a soft ball. Plunge the base of the pan into the cold water to stop the syrup cooking.
4 Mix together the cornflour and icing sugar in a large bowl with 100ml (3½fl oz) of the water. Bring the remaining water to the boil, then gradually beat into the cornflour mixture with a wooden spoon.
5 Pour the cornflour mixture into the pan and simmer until thickened, beating to ensure there are no lumps.
6 Gradually beat in the sugar syrup and simmer rapidly for about 30–35 minutes, stirring often, especially towards the end of the cooking time. The mixture should become very thick and turn pale golden.
7 Add the honey, chosen flavouring and food colouring and stir well. Turn out into the prepared tin and leave in a cool place overnight to set.
8 Lay a sheet of baking parchment on a work surface and dust liberally with a mixture of cornflour and icing sugar. Loosen the edges of the Turkish delight with a knife and turn out onto the parchment. Dust the top again and cut into squares. Toss well in the cornflour–icing sugar mixture. This Turkish delight keeps for up to two weeks in an airtight container or sealed packet.

RASPBERRY AND VANILLA MARSHMALLOWS

PREPARATION: *25 minutes,*
  plus setting
COOKING: *10 minutes*
MAKES: *about 60–70 pieces*

FOR THE RASPBERRY JELLY:
12g (⅓oz) leaf gelatine
250g (9oz) raspberries
1 tbsp icing sugar
pink food colouring paste

FOR THE MARSHMALLOW:
sunflower oil, for greasing
3 tbsp icing sugar and 3 tbsp
  cornflour combined, for dusting
500g (1lb 2oz) white granulated
  sugar
1 tbsp liquid glucose
200ml (7fl oz) water
22g (¾oz) leaf gelatine
2 medium egg whites
1 tsp vanilla extract

1 First make the raspberry jelly. Fill a bowl with cold water and soak the gelatine for 5 minutes. Cook the raspberries gently in a small pan with the icing sugar and a splash of water (they'll release their juices and collapse). Then, push through a sieve into a bowl and discard the pips.
2 Rinse the pan and heat the raspberry purée gently. Meanwhile, squeeze the excess water out of the gelatine and melt into the purée.
3 Fill a large bowl with ice and water and set the pan over it. Stir every so often to cool down the mixture – you need it to set enough so that it thickens but is still fluid enough to fold into the marshmallow.
4 To make the marshmallows. Fill the sink or a large bowl with cold water. Lightly oil a 23cm x 33cm (9in x 13in) tin. Dust the inside with 1 tablespoon each of sifted cornflour and icing sugar.
5 Over a low heat, melt the granulated sugar with the liquid glucose and water until the sugar has completely dissolved. Using a wet pastry brush, wash down the sides of the pan to dissolve any stray sugar crystals that may cause the sugar syrup to crystallise. Meanwhile, put the gelatine sheets into a bowl of cold water to soften, as before.
6 Bring the syrup to the boil – do not stir – and cook until a sugar thermometer measures 127°C/261°F (the hard ball stage). If you don't have a thermometer, drop a teaspoon of the mixture into a bowl of cold water. Bring it together with your fingers – it should form a hard ball. When it reaches the correct temperature, plunge the base of the pan into the sink of cold water to stop the syrup cooking.
7 Squeeze out the excess water from the gelatine and stir into the syrup.
8 Just before the sugar syrup reaches the correct temperature, whisk the egg whites until stiff, then whisk in the vanilla extract briefly. With the whisk still running, trickle in the sugar syrup. This is easier with a free-standing mixer but you could also whisk with an electric whisk if you have someone to help pour in the syrup. Whisk for about 10 minutes until the mixture holds its shape – it will be a thick white mass. Finally, whisk in a few dabs (or drops) of pink food colouring.

9 Swirl in the raspberry purée jelly so that it forms ripples. Pour into the prepared tin, smooth out and leave to set for several hours.

10 Liberally dust a large sheet of baking parchment with the cornflour and icing sugar mixture. Loosen the marshmallow at the edges with a flat-bladed knife and turn out on to the baking parchment.

11 Dust the top again and leave for 1 hour to form a crust. Cut into squares and toss in the icing sugar. This marshmallow keeps for up to two weeks in an airtight container or sealed packet.

These soft, pillowy marshmallows are rippled with a tangy raspberry jelly that looks pretty and tastes divine. Purists might prefer their marshmallow as plain vanilla, in which case simply omit the fruity part.

HONEY AND ALMOND NOUGAT

PREPARATION: *40 minutes, plus standing*

COOKING: *15 minutes*

MAKES: *64 pieces*

rice paper sheets
150g (5½oz) clear honey
250g (9oz) granulated sugar
1 tbsp liquid glucose
120ml (4fl oz) water
2 medium egg whites
1 tsp vanilla extract
150g (5½oz) almonds, warmed
120g (4oz) apricots, roughly chopped

This nougat will bring a smile to the face of any receiver as they bite into the wonderfully white gooey chewiness. I like to experiment when making this nougat – each time using a different honey, such as orange blossom, wildflower or lavender, or varying the nuts to include pistachios or macadamias instead.

1 Line a 20cm (7¾in) square tin with clingfilm, overlapping the sides of the tin. Cover the base with rice paper. Keep the honey warm in a small bowl set in a bowl of boiling water from the kettle. Fill the sink or a washing up bowl with cold water.

2 Put the sugar, glucose and the water into a medium-sized, heavy-bottomed pan and set over a low heat until the sugar is completely dissolved. Bring to the boil, without stirring, and cook until the mixture reaches 138°C/280°F on a sugar thermometer.

3 Stir in the honey and continue boiling until the temperature reaches 155°C/311°F. As it's approaching the critical temperature, whisk the egg whites in a free-standing mixer until stiff, ready for step 4. Once the syrup reaches 155°C/311°F, plunge the base of the pan into the sink or a bowl of cold water to stop the syrup cooking further.

4 While the motor of the mixer is running, carefully pour in the syrup in a thin stream into the stiff egg whites. Keep beating until the mixture is thick and holds its shape but is still pourable.

5 Next, beat in the vanilla. Then, fold in the warm nuts and chopped apricots and pour into the tin. Smooth out the top and cover with more rice paper. Fold over the clingfilm and put another baking tin with weights on top to weigh it down. Leave in a cool place overnight to set.

6 When set, cut into pieces (whatever size you like) and wrap in cellophane. This nougat keeps for up to two weeks in an airtight container or sealed packet.

TREACLE TOFFEE

PREPARATION: *30 minutes,*
  plus setting
COOKING: *20 minutes*
MAKES: *about 900g (2lb)*

100g (3½oz) unsalted butter,
  plus extra for greasing
500g (1lb 2oz) soft light brown
  sugar
1 tbsp liquid glucose
150ml (5fl oz) cold water
110g (3¾oz) black treacle
110g (3¾oz) golden syrup

Hands off kids! This toffee is
strictly for the grown-ups. The
strong, molasses-like flavour
comes from the black treacle.

1 Lightly grease a 24cm x 32cm (9½in x 12½in) baking tin, or one with similar dimensions; you could also use a silicone mould for round versions, as shown below. Fill the sink or a large bowl with cold water.
2 Put the sugar and liquid glucose in a large heavy-based pan with the water. Gently heat until the sugar has dissolved. Wash down the sides of the pan with a wet pastry brush to dissolve any sugar crystals.
3 When the sugar has completely dissolved, add the remaining ingredients and bring to the boil. Boil steadily without stirring until a sugar thermometer reaches 132°C/270°F (the soft crack stage). If you don't have a thermometer, drop a teaspoon of the mixture into a bowl of cold water. Bring it together with your fingers – it should form firm but pliable threads. When it reaches the correct temperature, dip the base of the pan into the sink of cold water to stop it cooking.
4 Pour into the prepared tin and leave to cool, marking into squares before it sets. Turn out the toffee when it is completely cold and break into squares. Wrap in coloured foil, lined with waxed paper or cellophane. This toffee keeps for up to a month in a cool place.

VANILLA CARAMELS

PREPARATION: *15 minutes,*
  plus setting
COOKING: *20 minutes*
MAKES: *about 700g (1lb 10oz)*

sunflower oil, for greasing
500g (1lb 2oz) granulated sugar
150ml (5fl oz) milk
120g (4oz) liquid glucose
200g (7oz) canned sweetened
  condensed milk
50g (1¾oz) butter, melted
¼ tsp vanilla extract

The warm, sweet notes of the vanilla will create wondrous aromas in your kitchen while you're making these super-sweet and chewy caramels. If you want another variation, then peppermint extract works well.

1 Grease an 18cm (7in) loose-bottomed square cake tin, and fill the sink or a large bowl with cold water.
2 Put the sugar and milk in a large heavy-bottomed pan and heat gently until the sugar has dissolved. Wash down the sides of the pan with a pastry brush dipped in water to dissolve any sugar crystals.
3 Add the liquid glucose and bring to the boil. Boil steadily without stirring until a sugar thermometer reaches 121°C/250°F (the firm ball stage). If you don't have a thermometer, drop a teaspoon of the mixture into a bowl of cold water. It should form a firm ball between your fingers.
4 Slowly pour in the condensed milk, butter and vanilla extract and stir to combine. Continue boiling to 124°C/255°F (the hard ball stage). Immediately dip the base of the pan into the cold water, then pour the caramel mixture into the prepared tin. Leave to set for a short time before marking into fingers, squares or bars.
5 Turn out the caramels when completely cold and, using oiled scissors, cut into 6cm x 1cm (2½in x ½in) fingers, then wrap in cellophane. These caramels keep for up to a month in a cool place.

PEANUT BRITTLE

Whether you like to snap a sweet nutty piece onto ice cream or just nibble on some when you feel the need, this brittle also makes a perfect foodie gift. Don't feel wedded to peanuts, though; toasted almonds, macadamias or pistachios are all admirable substitutes.

PREPARATION: *15 minutes,*
  plus cooling
COOKING: *20 minutes*
MAKES: *about 625g (1lb 6oz)*

75g (2¾oz) *unsalted butter, plus*
  extra for greasing
400g (14oz) *salted, roasted*
  peanuts
425g (15oz) *granulated sugar*
150g (5½oz) *soft light brown*
  sugar
175g (6¼oz) *golden syrup*
150ml (5fl oz) *water*

1 Liberally grease a baking sheet or a marble slab measuring about 30cm x 40cm (12in x 16in). Preheat the oven to 130°C/250°F/gas mark ½.
2 Sprinkle the nuts on to a baking sheet and keep warm in the oven.
3 Put the butter, sugars and golden syrup into a large deep pan along with the water. Gently heat until the sugar has dissolved. Wash down the sides of the pan with a pastry brush dipped in water to dissolve any sugar crystals.
4 When the sugar is completely dissolved, bring to the boil. Boil steadily without stirring until a sugar thermometer reaches 149°C/300°F (the hard crack stage). If you don't have a thermometer, drop a teaspoon of the mixture into a bowl of cold water and it should snap easily.
5 Quickly and thoroughly stir in the warmed nuts. Pour the mixture onto the greased baking sheet or slab and spread out thinly. Leave to cool completely, then break into pieces. This brittle keeps for up to two weeks in an airtight container or sealed packet.

PEANUT BUTTER FUDGE

PREPARATION: *20 minutes,*
plus standing
COOKING: *10 minutes*
MAKES: *about 800g (1lb 12¼oz)*

500g (1lb 2oz) granulated sugar
1 tbsp glucose syrup
150ml (5fl oz) Jersey or whole
  milk
150g (5½oz) unsalted butter
150g (5½oz) crunchy peanut
  butter

If you like your sweets with a savoury edge, then this fudge is for you. I use a crunchy peanut butter to give it an interesting texture, but use a smooth version if you prefer your fudge silky smooth.

1 Line a 13cm x 18cm (5in x 7in) baking tin or dish with clingfilm so that it overlaps the edges. Fill a large bowl or the sink with cold water.

2 Put all of the ingredients in a heavy-bottomed pan and heat very gently until the sugar is completely dissolved – take your time and make sure all the grains are melted; otherwise the fudge won't be smooth. Use a wet pastry brush to wash down the sides of the pan to dissolve any stray sugar crystals that may cause the sugar syrup to crystallise while cooking.

3 Bring to the boil and continue bubbling, stirring occasionally to ensure the mixture isn't catching on the base, until it reaches 116°C/241°F (the soft ball stage) on a sugar thermometer. If you don't have a thermometer, drop a teaspoon of the mixture into a bowl of cold water. Bring it together with your fingers – it should form a soft ball.

4 Immediately plunge the base of the pan into the cold water to stop the fudge cooking. Transfer the pan to a cold surface and leave to stand for 5 minutes – it's important to do this otherwise the texture of the fudge will become crumbly rather than smooth.

5 Beat the fudge mixture with an electric whisk for 5–10 minutes until thick, then quickly tip into the prepared tin and smooth the surface.

6 When completely cold, cut into squares or bars. This fudge keeps for up to a month in an airtight container or sealed packet.

COFFEE AND CARDAMOM FUDGE

PREPARATION: *20 minutes,*
plus standing
COOKING: *30 minutes*
MAKES: *about 35 pieces*

unsalted butter, for greasing
700g (1lb 10oz) granulated
sugar
175ml (6fl oz) water
397g (14oz) canned sweetened
condensed milk
110g (3¾oz) salted butter
2 tsp instant coffee powder
mixed with 1 tbsp hot water
1 tsp cardamom seeds, ground

I've paired cardamom with this crumbly coffee fudge to balance the taste, and the fantastically aromatic cardamom is just heavenly.

1 Grease a 13cm x 18cm (5in x 7in) non-stick tin. Fill the sink or a large bowl with cold water.

2 Put all of the ingredients (discard the cardamom pods) in a heavy-bottomed pan and heat very gently until the sugar has completely dissolved – take your time and make sure all the grains are melted otherwise the fudge won't be smooth. I use a wet pastry brush to wash down the sides of the pan to dissolve any stray sugar crystals that may cause the sugar syrup to crystallise while cooking.

3 Raise the heat and steadily boil the syrup to 116°C/241°F (the soft ball stage) on a sugar thermometer. If you don't have a thermometer, drop a teaspoon of the mixture into a bowl of cold water. Bring it together with your fingers – it should form a soft ball. Take the pan straight off the heat and dip the base in cold water.

4 Let the sugar syrup rest for a minute or two, then with a wooden spoon, stir in the cardamom seeds. Continue stirring until the fudge starts to grain and stiffen (you will feel the consistency change against your wooden spoon), then pour into the prepared tin.

5 While still warm, mark into squares, then cut into pieces when completely cold. This fudge keeps for up to a month when stored in an airtight container, separated by layers of greaseproof paper.

SESAME SNAPS

PREPARATION: *5 minutes*
COOKING: *25–30 minutes*
MAKES: *about 550g (1lb 3½oz)*

sunflower oil, for greasing
200g (7oz) sesame seeds
400g (14oz) granulated sugar
1 tbsp liquid glucose
100ml (3½fl oz) water

For easy packaging, I've made my sesame snaps in small pieces but you could just crack the big sheet into shards for more dramatic packages. I like the size of sesame seeds, but I've found it works well with sunflower seeds, too.

1 Grease a marble slab or heavy baking sheet with oil, and fill the sink or a large bowl with cold water.
2 Put a large frying pan over a medium-low heat and dry fry the sesame seeds until lightly golden and nutty smelling – watch them like a hawk to make sure they don't burn. Keep warm.
3 Put the sugar and water into a small heavy-bottomed pan and heat gently until the sugar has dissolved. Wash down the sides of the pan with a pastry brush dipped in water to dissolve any sugar crystals.
4 Boil steadily without stirring until a sugar thermometer reaches 149°C/300°F (the hard crack stage – it will have a yellowish tinge). If you don't have a thermometer, drop a teaspoon of the mixture into a bowl of cold water. It should snap easily between your fingers. Then, plunge the base of the pan into the cold water.
5 Quickly mix in the sesame seeds and pour onto the prepared surface. When cold, snap into pieces. These snaps keep for up to a month between layers of waxed paper in an airtight container or sealed packet.

FRUIT SALAMI

PREPARATION: *40 minutes,*
 plus maturing
COOKING: *5–10 minutes*
MAKES: *about 825g (1lb 13oz),*
 one salami

225g (8oz) dried apricots,
 chopped
225g (8oz) dried figs, chopped
2 tbsp apricot brandy (or normal
 brandy)
100g (3½oz) walnuts, toasted
 and finely chopped
100g (3½oz) candied peel
rice paper, for wrapping

A sweet 'salami' – or *salame dolce* – is a speciality of southern Italy.
It looks like a salami but tastes like fruity heaven. I like to serve this
delicious 'salami' in slices with coffee or a dessert wine or as part of
a cheeseboard. *Delizioso*, as the Italians like to say.

1 Preheat the oven to 170°C/325°F/gas mark 3. Meanwhile, whizz the
apricots and figs in a food processor to make a sticky paste. Mix in the
brandy and transfer the mixture to a bowl.
2 Toast the walnuts on a baking sheet for 5–10 minutes. Remove from
the oven, allow to cool and chop finely. Mix in the peel and walnuts.
3 Put a large piece of baking parchment on a work surface. Transfer the
mixture to the parchment and, using the paper, shape the mixture into
a 'sausage' about 30cm (12in) long and 6cm (2½in) thick.
4 Next, put a piece of rice paper on a work surface and put the 'sausage'
on one long end. Roll up tightly and trim any excess. Roll in greaseproof
paper and twist the ends. Store in a cool place for a month before eating.

TOFFEE APPLES

PREPARATION: *30 minutes*
COOKING: *15 minutes*
MAKES: *12*

12 small dessert apples, stalks
  removed
12 lolly sticks
sunflower oil, for greasing
500g (1lb 2oz) demerara sugar
120ml (4fl oz) cold water
1 tsp white wine vinegar
5 tbsp golden syrup

What could be a better
treat for Halloween
or Bonfire Night party
bags than a super-sweet
crunchy toffee apple?
They're hard to beat.

1 Put the apples in a large bowl and briefly cover with boiling water to remove their wax coating. It will also help the sugar syrup to stick to the fruit. Drain and dry thoroughly with kitchen paper. Push a lolly stick through the base of each apple into the core and set aside.

2 Oil a large baking sheet and place on the work surface as near to the hob as possible. Fill the sink with cold water.

3 Put the sugar in a large pan with the water. Gently heat until the sugar has dissolved. Wash down the sides of the pan with a pastry brush dipped in water to dissolve any sugar crystals.

4 When the sugar has completely dissolved, add the vinegar and golden syrup and bring to the boil. Boil steadily without stirring until a sugar thermometer reaches 140°C/284°C (the soft crack stage). If you don't have a thermometer, drop a teaspoon of the mixture into a bowl of cold water. Bring it together with your fingers – it should form firm but pliable threads. When it reaches the correct temperature, plunge the base of the pan into the cold water to stop the toffee cooking.

5 Dip the apples into the toffee, tilting the pan and twisting the stick so that they are completely covered. Hold each apple over the pan for a few seconds to allow the excess toffee to drip off. Put each apple on the baking parchment to set. Do not touch until the toffee coating is completely cold. Wrap each toffee apple in cellophane and store in a cool, dry place (not the fridge) and eat within five days.

ROSEHIP CREAMS

PREPARATION: *25 minutes,*
  plus drying
MAKES: 20–22

225g (8oz) icing sugar, sifted
4 tsp rosehip syrup
finely grated zest and juice of
  ½ lemon
pink food colouring paste

These delicate pink, scented creams make the most of an ingredient that is rarely thought of – the rosehip. I use rosehip syrup here but if you live near hedgerows, then why not make some rosehip syrup yourself.

1 Put the icing sugar in a bowl. Add the rosehip syrup, lemon zest and enough juice to make a stiff paste. Then, add enough pink food colouring to delicately tint the paste.

2 Dust the work surface with icing sugar and knead until smooth and evenly coloured. Roll out to a 5mm (¼in) thicknesss. Using a 3.5cm (1½in) round cutter, stamp out circles, re-rolling any trimmings. Leave the discs to dry on a sheet of baking parchment for one to three days until dry to the touch (this will depend on the weather!).

3 Pop into petit-four cases. These creams keep for up to four weeks in an airtight container or sealed packet.

Something for
the storecupboard

STEM GINGER IN SYRUP

Choose smooth, plump-looking
ginger for the best flavour. It will
also be less fibrous.

PREPARATION: *25 minutes*
COOKING: *1 hour*
MAKES: *about 800g (1lb 12¼oz)*

500g (1lb 2oz) root ginger
1kg (2¼lb) granulated sugar
1 tbsp liquid glucose
1 litre (1¾ pints) water

1 The easiest way to peel the ginger is to use the
edge of a teaspoon to scrape away the skin – it will
enable you to get into the knobbly corners better
than any vegetable peeler.
2 Cut the peeled ginger into roughly equal-sized
cubes. Put into a pan and cover with cold water.
Bring to the boil, then simmer for 10 minutes. Drain,
recover with water, bring to the boil and simmer
again for 10 minutes. Drain and set aside.
3 In another pan, heat the sugar and liquid glucose
with the water. Heat gently to dissolve the sugar,

brushing the sides of the pan with a wet pastry brush.
4 Add the ginger and boil steadily without stirring
until a sugar thermometer reaches 108°C/226°F (the
thread stage); this should take about 30 minutes.
Alternatively, if you don't have a thermometer, take a
teaspoon of the mixture and hold the spoon sideways
over a saucer. It should drip as a thin thread.
5 Put the ginger and syrup into sterilised jars, seal
and label. This preserve keeps indefinitely.

FLAVOURED SALTS

**FOR THE MIDDLE EASTERN
SALT:**

120g (4oz) sea salt

1 tsp smoked paprika

1 tsp dried chilli flakes

*2 tsp cumin seeds, lightly
toasted in a dry pan*

FOR THE SCANDINAVIAN SALT:

120g (4oz) sea salt

1½ tsp dried dill

*12 juniper berries, crushed and
roughly chopped*

**FOR THE MEDITERRANEAN
SALT:**

120g (4oz) sea salt

1½ tsp dried oregano

finely grated zest of 2 lemons

A salt with infused flavours can raise a humble dish to the realms of a princely one, whether added at the end of cooking or right at the beginning. The ones here are my favourites, but once you've made these why not experiment with other flavours? It's important to use a good-quality sea salt for this recipe – standard table salt may be cheaper but it won't taste half as good.

1 Put each set of ingredients into a separate bowl and stir together thoroughly.

2 Decant into jars, seal, label and attach a wooden salt spoon to each.

CRANBERRY, ORANGE AND GINGER CHUTNEY

PREPARATION: *20 minutes,*
  plus maturing
COOKING: *35 minutes*
MAKES: *about 1.2kg (2½lb)*

5cm (2in) piece root ginger, sliced
1 small cinnamon stick, broken
3 whole cloves
500g (1lb 2oz) fresh cranberries
500g (1lb 2oz) Bramley apples,
  peeled, cored and chopped
120g (4oz) dried cranberries
finely grated zest and juice of
  1 orange
300g (10½oz) granulated sugar
400ml (13½fl oz) white wine
  vinegar

Of course, this chutney is the perfect traditional accompaniment to roast turkey but it also tastes great with Swedish-style meatballs or slices of cold ham. I also stir it into a venison casserole at the end of cooking to add a fruity note.

1 Cut out a 12cm (4½in) square of muslin and put the ginger and spices in the centre. Bring together the corners and tie firmly with a piece of kitchen string.

2 Put the muslin bag and the remaining ingredients into a preserving pan or large saucepan. Heat gently until the sugar is dissolved.

3 Bring to the boil, then lower the heat to a simmer and cook for 30 minutes until thickened. To tell if the chutney is ready, draw a wooden spoon across the base of the pan – it should leave a visible channel for 1–2 seconds.

4 While the chutney is still hot, decant into hot, sterilised jars, cover with a disc of waxed paper and seal with vinegar-proof lids.

5 Label when cold and leave to mature in a cool, dark place for a month before eating. This chutney keeps for up to a year unopened. Once it's opened, refrigerate and use within four weeks.

Add its many uses to the label so the recipient of your gift can enjoy it whenever they like.

THAI GREEN CURRY PASTE

PREPARATION: *25 minutes*
COOKING: *2 minutes*
MAKES: *about 320g (11¼oz)*

1 tsp cumin seeds
2 tsp coriander seeds
6 large green chillies, roughly
  chopped, including seeds
2 shallots, roughly chopped
5cm (2in) piece galangal or root
  ginger, peeled and chopped
3 garlic cloves, crushed
2 stalks lemongrass, trimmed
  and chopped
50g (1¾oz) fresh coriander,
  leaves and stalks, roughly
  chopped
finely grated zest and juice of
  2 limes
3 tbsp sunflower oil
2 tsp fish sauce

This aromatic and vibrant curry paste is simple to make and really packs a punch in the flavour stakes. What's more, it's totally adaptable and can make the base of any curry you happen to like – meat, fish or vegetable.

1 Put a small pan over a medium heat and dry fry the cumin and coriander seeds for a minute or so until lightly toasted and aromatic – don't leave the pan unattended for even a moment as they burn easily. Allow to cool for a few minutes.
2 Put all of the remaining ingredients into a food processor with the cooled seeds and whizz to a coarse purée – but make sure that all the ingredients, particularly the fibrous lemongrass, are properly processed.
3 Divide the paste between sterilised jars, seal and label. This paste keeps for two weeks in the fridge.

HARISSA PASTE

PREPARATION: *20 minutes,*
  plus soaking
COOKING: *5 minutes*
MAKES: *about 70g (2½oz)*

50g (1¾oz) dried chillies
1 tsp caraway seeds
½ tsp cumin seeds
1 tsp coriander seeds
2 garlic cloves, roughly chopped
juice of ¼ lemon
½ tsp salt
3–4 tbsp olive oil, plus extra for
  covering

Harissa is a wonderfully versatile paste – it's spicy and fragrant – and can transform stews or soups, can be used as a rub for meat or poultry or simply stirred into yogurt or couscous. It's powerful, though, so package in small spice jars as a little goes a long way.

1 Put the chillies into a bowl and cover with boiling water. Leave to soak for an hour.
2 Dry fry the whole spices in a small pan over a medium heat for a few minutes until toasted and they smell aromatic. Keep a close watch on them so that they don't burn.
3 Drain the chillies, discarding the water. Put into a food processor with the toasted spices, garlic, lemon juice and salt, and blend to a paste.
4 Blend in enough of the oil to loosen the mixture slightly. Transfer to sterilised jars, leaving a small gap at the top. Cover with a thin layer of oil. Seal and label. This paste keeps for up to four months.

SPICY LIME PICKLE

PREPARATION: *25 minutes,*
  plus maturing
COOKING: *5 minutes*
MAKES: *about 1.8kg (4lb)*

500ml (18fl oz) white wine
  vinegar
400g (14oz) granulated sugar
juice of 2 limes
12 limes, each cut into 6 wedges
40g (1½oz) salt
5 whole dried chillies
2.5cm (1in) piece root ginger, cut
  into slices

Move over mango chutney, it's time to try and savour this spicy pickle. This classic Indian accompaniment often gets overlooked but once you've tried it – the limes are so flavoursome – you'll be making batches to persuade everyone to fly the flag for this delicious Indian preserve.

1 Put the vinegar and sugar into a large pan. Heat gently until the sugar has dissolved. Add the lime juice and boil for 2 minutes. Leave to cool for 10 minutes.
2 Pack the limes tightly into hot, sterilised jars, layering with salt, chillies and ginger as you do so.
3 Pour the vinegar mixture into the jars, making sure the limes are completely covered. To stop them bobbing above the surface of the liquid, tuck a wedge of folded greaseproof paper on the top. Seal and leave in a cool, dark place for six weeks before eating.

SWEET AND SPICY MANGO CHUTNEY

PREPARATION: *35 minutes*
COOKING: *35 minutes*
MAKES: *about 500g (1lb 2oz)*

½ tsp cumin seeds
½ tsp dried flaked chillies
250ml (8½fl oz) cider vinegar
200g (7oz) soft brown sugar
1kg (2¼lb) ripe mangoes, peeled,
  stoned and chopped
1 tsp nigella seeds

I use Alphonso mangoes to make this chutney. They only have a short season but are deeply aromatic and have an intense peachy, honeyed flavour. It doesn't matter if you can't find this variety, though, as the chutney will still be delicious. I have tried making this chutney in larger batches but the cooking time has to increase and I find it loses its freshness – but if you don't mind that, then feel free to double or triple the recipe quantities below.

1 Put a small pan over a medium heat. Dry-cook the cumin seeds for 30 seconds to 1 minute, shaking the pan often. Be careful not to burn them and don't leave them unattended.
2 Put the cumin seeds and the remaining ingredients, except for the nigella seeds, into a preserving pan or large deep pan and set over a low heat until the sugar has dissolved.
3 Bring to the boil, then lower the heat to a simmer and cook for 30 minutes until thickened. To tell if the chutney is ready, draw a wooden spoon across the base of the pan – it should leave a visible channel for 1–2 seconds. Now, stir in the nigella seeds.
4 While the chutney is still hot, decant into hot, sterilised jars, cover with discs of waxed paper and seal with vinegar-proof lids. Label when cold. You can enjoy this chutney the next day, but it will keep for up to a year unopened. Refrigerate after opening and use within four weeks.

Preserving jars come in a wonderful array of clipdown tops for perfect preserves every time.

RIGHT *(clockwise from front left) Thai green curry paste, Spicy lime pickle, Sweet and spicy mango chutney and Cranberry, orange and ginger chutney.* **LEFT** *Harissa paste.*

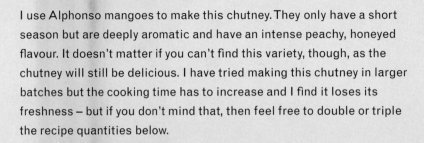

A home-made mustard really packs a great punch. Here you can try just one or all three for slightly different flavour combinations. I source large packs of mustard seeds from Asian food stores.

FOR THE CHILLI AND GARLIC MUSTARD:

100g (3½oz) black mustard seeds

50g (1¾oz) yellow mustard seeds

120ml (4fl oz) white wine vinegar

2 tsp chilli flakes

2 tsp paprika

3 garlic cloves, crushed

1 tsp salt

A TRIO OF MUSTARDS

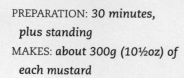

PREPARATION: *30 minutes,*
  plus standing
MAKES: *about 300g (10½oz) of*
  each mustard

FOR THE WHOLEGRAIN HONEY MUSTARD:

100g (3½oz) black mustard seeds
50g (1¾oz) yellow mustard seeds
120ml (4fl oz) white wine vinegar
2 tbsp clear honey
1 tsp salt

FOR THE TARRAGON MUSTARD:

50g (1¾oz) black mustard seeds
100g (3½oz) yellow mustard
  seeds
120ml (4fl oz) cider vinegar
1 shallot, finely chopped
1 tbsp tarragon leaves,
  chopped
1 tsp salt

1 Whichever mustard you want to make, they all start off in the same way. Put the mustard seeds in a non-metallic bowl, pour in the vinegar, cover and leave to stand for 24 hours at room temperature.

2 Stir the rest of the flavourings into each bowl, or whichever you're making. Add a drop more vinegar if the mixture seems too dry. Now, you can leave the seeds whole as they are in the mustard or put the mixture into a food processor and blend for a minute or two to break some of them down. I prefer to do the latter as it makes a creamier mustard.

3 Whichever method you choose, decant the mustards into small jars, seal with vinegar-proof lids and leave to mature for at least two weeks to allow the flavours to mingle. These mustards keep for up to a year unopened. Once they're opened, use within two months.

From the garden

Make a personalised and
hand-stamped label.
Simply clip onto some
string with a mini peg.

THIS PAGE *(clockwise from top) Spicy piccalilli, Spicy barbecue sauce and Pumpkin relish.*

SPICY PICCALILLI

PREPARATION: *30 minutes,*
  plus salting
COOKING: *25 minutes*
MAKES: *about 2kg (4½lb)*

2.5kg (5½lb) mixed vegetables,
  such as cauliflower, French
  beans, runner beans, shallots
cooking salt
30g (1¼oz) cornflour
1.5 litres (2 pints 10fl oz)
  distilled white vinegar
1 tbsp ground turmeric
1 tbsp dry English mustard
1 tbsp ground ginger
150g (5½oz) granulated sugar
½ tsp dried chilli flakes

Piccalilli is the English version of spiced Indian vegetables and is a great way of using up a glut of summer vegetables. Enjoy with a wedge of pork pie, cold meats or tangy cheeses for a simple lunch or Christmas day evening supper.

1 Cut the vegetables into bite-sized pieces. Put in a colander, layering with plenty of salt as you go (sit the colander on the draining board or on a plate to collect the juices). Put a plate on top and weigh it down with heavy tins. Leave to stand for 24 hours.

2 Quickly rinse the salt off the vegetables under running water and pat dry with kitchen paper.

3 Mix the cornflour with 2 tablespoons of the vinegar and set aside.

4 Put the remaining ingredients in a large pan. Stir together then add the vegetables. Bring to the boil, then simmer for 5–10 minutes until the vegetables are only just tender – keep checking with the point of a knife as they mustn't overcook and should still have some crunch to them.

5 Using a slotted spoon, remove the vegetables and pack them into hot, sterilised jars. Stir the cornflour mixture into the cooking liquid. Bring to the boil and simmer for 3–5 minutes, stirring, until it has slightly thickened.

6 Pour the vinegar mixture over the vegetables and seal with vinegar-proof lids. Store in a cool, dark place for a month before eating. This glorious pickle keeps for up to a year unopened. Once opened, though, it should be eaten within four weeks.

BARBECUE SAUCE

PREPARATION: *10 minutes*
COOKING: *30–35 minutes*
MAKES: *about 450ml (15¾fl oz)*

2 tbsp sunflower oil
1 medium onion, finely chopped
150ml (5fl oz) tomato ketchup
1 tsp cayenne pepper
3 tbsp Worcestershire sauce
150ml (5fl oz) cider vinegar
2 tbsp clear honey
1 tsp Dijon mustard
1 star anise

This wonderfully versatile sauce can be used as a condiment itself or brushed onto meat and poultry during cooking to add tangy spicy notes.

1 Heat the sunflower oil in a pan and gently fry the onion for 20 minutes until soft.
2 Add the remaining ingredients, bring to the boil and then simmer for 5 minutes. Cool slightly.
3 Remove the star anise and discard. Blend in a food processor or blender until very smooth. Pour into sterilised bottles and seal, then label. This spicy sauce keeps for up to two months. Refrigerate after opening and use within four weeks. Shake before use.

PUMPKIN RELISH

PREPARATION: *20 minutes*
COOKING: *1 hour*
MAKES: *about 800g (1lb 12¼oz)*

1kg (2¼lb) pumpkin or
  butternut squash, peeled,
  deseeded and diced
1 large onion, chopped
150g (5½oz) dark brown soft
  sugar
1 tsp celery seeds
1 tsp fennel seeds
360ml (12fl oz) cider vinegar

Take full advantage of the bumper bounty of pumpkins and squash in the autumn to make this delicious relish. I like to serve with some piquant cheese and 'warm from the oven' bread.

1 Put all of the ingredients into a large deep pan or a preserving pan and set over a low heat until the sugar has dissolved.
2 Bring to the boil, then lower the heat to a simmer and cook for about 45–60 minutes until the pumpkin is tender but not disintegrated.
3 While the relish is still hot, decant into hot, sterilised jars, cover with discs of waxed paper (the waxy side should be relish side down) and seal with vinegar-proof lids. Label when cold. Store in a cool, dry place for a month before eating. This relish keeps for up to a year unopened. Refrigerate after opening and use within four weeks.

GOOSEBERRY CHUTNEY

PREPARATION: *25 minutes*
COOKING: *1 hour 30 minutes*
MAKES: *about 1.3kg (2lb 14oz)*

3 slices root ginger
1 tsp coriander seeds
6 black peppercorns
1.4kg (3lb 1½oz) cooking
 gooseberries, topped and tailed
350g (12oz) raisins
225g (8oz) red onions, finely
 chopped
225g (8oz) soft brown sugar
600ml (1 pint) white wine
 vinegar

One of my favourite lunches is home-made bread, a good tangy cheese and a dollop of my gooseberry chutney. I think it would make a pleasing gift for any food lover.

1 Lay out a 12cm (4½in) square of muslin on a work surface and put the ginger and spices in the centre. Draw the corners together and fasten with some kitchen string.
2 Put the remaining ingredients along with the spice bag into a preserving pan or large deep pan and set over a low heat until the sugar has dissolved.
3 Bring to the boil, then lower the heat to a simmer and cook for 1 hour–1 hour 30 minutes until thickened. To tell if the chutney is ready, draw a wooden spoon across the base of the pan – it should leave a visible channel for 1–2 seconds. Remove and discard the spice bag.
4 While the chutney is still hot, decant into hot, sterilised jars, cover with discs of waxed paper (the waxy side should be chutney side down) and seal with vinegar-proof lids. Label when cold. Store in a cool, dry place for a month before eating. This chutney keeps for up to a year unopened. Refrigerate after opening and use within four weeks.

Tying on a vintage spoon means the gift can be enjoyed as soon as it's unwrapped.

RIGHT *(from left to right) Gooseberry chutney, Fig relish and Sweet chilli sauce.*

SWEET CHILLI SAUCE

PREPARATION: **15 minutes**
COOKING: **30 minutes**
MAKES: **650ml (1 pint 2fl oz)**

500g (1lb 2oz) granulated sugar
600ml (1 pint) water
6 large red chillies
1 tbsp dried chilli flakes
150ml (5fl oz) rice vinegar
3 garlic cloves, crushed
1 tbsp fish sauce
2 tbsp cornflour

Here's one for all lovers of Thai flavours. The enduring partnership of sweet and spicy is a winner and I like to use this fiery and delicious sauce as a marinade or as a dipping sauce for Thai fish cakes.

1 Put the sugar into a large pan with the water and heat gently until the sugar has dissolved completely.
2 Add the remaining ingredients, except the cornflour, and bring to the boil. Lower the heat to a simmer and bubble for about 30 minutes until the sauce is lightly syrupy.
3 Put the cornflour into a small bowl and stir in a spoonful or two of the chilli sauce to blend into a paste. Tip back into the pan and bring to the boil, stirring constantly. Cook for 1–2 minutes.
4 Using a sterilised funnel, pour into sterilised bottles, seal and then label when cold. This sauce keeps for up to a year. Once opened, store it in the fridge and use within three months. Shake before use.

FIG RELISH

PREPARATION: *40 minutes*
COOKING: *1 hour*
MAKES: *about 875g (1lb 14¾oz)*

1 tbsp sunflower oil
225g (8oz) onions, finely
   chopped
4 black peppercorns
1 star anise
450g (1lb) fresh figs, chopped
400g (14oz) Bramley apples,
   peeled and cored
finely grated zest and juice of
   1 orange
225g (8oz) soft dark brown
   sugar
200ml (7fl oz) cider vinegar
½ tsp salt

As this relish has a shorter cooking time, it doesn't keep for as long.
It's marvellous with a crumbly Lancashire cheese.

1 In a large deep pan, heat the oil and gently fry the onions for
10 minutes until softened.
2 Lay out a 12cm (4½in) square of muslin on a work surface and put the
spices in the centre. Draw the corners together and fasten with string.
3 Put the remaining ingredients, along with the spice bag, into the pan
and set over a low heat until the sugar has dissolved.
4 Bring to the boil, then lower the heat to a simmer and cook for
35–40 minutes until thickened. To tell if the chutney is ready, draw
a wooden spoon across the base of the pan – it should leave a visible
channel for 1–2 seconds. When it's ready, discard the spice bag.
5 While the chutney is still hot, decant into hot, sterilised jars, cover
with a disc of waxed paper and seal with vinegar-proof lids then label
when cold. Store in a cool, dry place for a month before eating. This
relish keeps for up to six months unopened but once opened it should
be refrigerated and used within four weeks.

ASIAN-SPICED VEGETABLES

A riot of colour in a jar is the first thing you see of these preserved vegetables, but their taste packs a punch, too. With its Oriental flavours singing loud, this is an unusual and impressive gift for anyone who loves food from the Far East.

1 Slice the vegetables finely with a mandolin or sharp knife. Pack into sterilised jars in layers.

2 Put the vinegar in a pan along with the ginger, pepper, chilli and the water. Bring to the boil then pour over the vegetables, making sure they are fully covered.

3 Seal with vinegar-proof lids and label. Store in a cool, dark place for one month before using. These spiced vegetables keep for six months.

PICKLED ONIONS

PREPARATION: *60 minutes, plus soaking and maturing*
COOKING: *2 minutes*
MAKES: *about 1.7kg (3lb 15oz)*

1 litre (1¾ pints) distilled vinegar
1 tsp fennel seeds
1 tsp celery seeds
1 tsp black peppercorns
4 bay leaves
1 tsp yellow mustard seeds
1 tsp blade mace
75g (2¾oz) cooking salt
600ml (1 pint) boiling water
750g (1lb 11¾oz) pickling onions, peeled and left whole

All that is needed to accompany these feisty crunchy pickles for a splendid supper is a crusty loaf, strong cheese and a good cider.

1 Put all of the ingredients, except the salt, boiling water and onions, into a stainless steel pan. Cover and heat gently until just under boiling point. Remove from the heat and leave to infuse overnight.

2 Put the salt into a large non-metallic bowl and cover with the measured boiling water. Stir to dissolve and leave this brine to cool.

3 Cover the onions with boiling water. Leave to stand for a couple of minutes, then drain and peel.

4 Add the onions to the brine, cover and leave for two days.

5 Drain the onions, rinse and pack tightly into sterilised jars. Drain the pickling vinegar, discarding the spices and pour over the onions, covering them completely. Seal and label. Leave for at least three months before eating. These onions keep for up to a year unopened. Once opened, use within two months.

PREPARATION: 20 minutes,
   plus sitting
MAKES: 1.8kg (4lb)

2 red peppers
3 carrots
1 red onion
1 mooli
¼ white cabbage

850ml (1½ pints) Japanese rice
   vinegar
2.5cm (1in) piece root ginger,
   peeled and sliced
1 tbsp Sichuan peppers
1 tsp chilli flakes
500ml (18fl oz) water

PLUM CHEESE

PREPARATION: *30 minutes*
COOKING: *1 hour 5 minutes*
MAKES: *about 800g (1lb 12¼oz)*

1kg (2¼lb) plums, quartered
granulated sugar

The slightly tart purple plums
that are available year round
work particularly well as a
fruit cheese. Serve as an
accompaniment to duck and
game or with a wedge of mature
Cheddar, the kind that tickles
the roof of your mouth.

1 Put the plums into a large deep pan and cover with water – there's
no need to peel or stone them. Bring to the boil, then simmer for
20 minutes until the fruit is very soft. Skim away any of the skin or
stones that rise to the surface.
2 Push the plums and the juices through a sieve, getting as much purée
as you can. Measure the purée and allow 350g (12oz) sugar for every
600ml (1 pint) you obtain.
3 Put the purée and sugar into a non-stick pan and heat slowly to
dissolve the sugar. Turn up the heat and boil for about 45 minutes until
the mixture is thick – a wooden spoon drawn across the bottom of the
pan should leave a clean line.
4 Transfer the cheese into a lightly oiled square or rectangular mould
(I find that disposable foil containers work well, too). Alternatively, use
small jars or dishes and cover with a disc of waxed paper. Cover the
containers or seal the jars and leave the cheese for two months before
eating. Wrap in waxed paper and decorate to give as a gift. This cheese
keeps for up to a year unopened. Once opened, use within two months.

QUINCE JELLY

PREPARATION: *30 minutes*
COOKING: *1 hour 10 minutes*
MAKES: *about 1kg (2¼lb)*

2.5kg (5½lb) quince
5 whole cloves
2 litres (3½ pints) water
granulated sugar

Despite looking like a cross between an apple and a pear, quinces straight from the bush are inedible. A short cooking journey transforms them into a delightful pink jelly that's delicious with duck and game or with cheese. A spoonful of this jelly stirred into gravies and savoury sauces adds a pleasing depth of flavour, too.

1 Roughly chop the quince into 3cm (1¼in) chunks – there's no need to peel or core them, everything goes into the pan.
2 Put the fruit into a preserving pan with the cloves and the water. Bring to the boil then simmer for about 1 hour until very soft and pulpy.
3 Carefully pour the quince and the liquid into a jelly bag and leave to strain overnight – do not be tempted to extract more juice by pushing down the mixture as it will make the jelly cloudy.
4 Measure the liquid: for every 600ml (1 pint) you will need 450g (1lb) of sugar. Put the juice and sugar into a preserving pan and heat gently to dissolve the sugar. Bring to the boil and boil for 5–10 minutes until setting point is reached, but I'd check after 5 minutes. To test, put a teaspoon of jelly onto a cold saucer, leave it to cool for a few minutes then push it with your finger. If it's reached setting point, it should wrinkle. If not continue boiling and testing until setting point is reached.
5 Skim any scum from the surface with a slotted spoon and transfer the jelly into hot, sterilised jars and seal. Label when cold. This jelly keeps for up to a year unopened. Once opened, use within three months.

RED ONION MARMALADE

PREPARATION: *25 minutes*
COOKING: *1 hour 30 minutes*
MAKES: *about 575g (1lb 4oz)*

1kg (2¼lb) red onions
2 tbsp olive oil
1 tsp salt
175g (6¼oz) soft light brown
  sugar
150ml (5fl oz) red wine
1 tbsp sherry vinegar
1 tbsp redcurrant jelly

I wouldn't be without a jar of this magical marmalade in my cupboard. It has myriad uses, from livening up a sandwich, enhancing a casserole or just to smother over sausages.

1 Using a mandolin or sharp knife, slice the onions very thinly. Heat the oil in a wide frying pan and add the onions along with the salt. Cover the onions with a circle of dampened greaseproof paper and a tightly fitting lid. Cook on the lowest heat for about 1 hour, stirring occasionally, until the onions are meltingly tender.
2 Discard the paper, turn up the heat and stir in the sugar. Cook, stirring often, until the liquid has evaporated and the onions are a deep brown colour (but not burned).
3 Pour in the wine and bubble until the liquid has evaporated, then stir in the redcurrant jelly and check the seasoning.
4 Divide between sterilised jars while still hot, seal and then label when cold. This condiment keeps for up to a year unopened. Once opened, store it in the fridge and use within six weeks.

Create a beautiful box of goodies to accompany this savoury marmalade.

SUNBLUSH TOMATOES

PREPARATION: *15 minutes,*
  plus draining
COOKING: *8–10 hours*
MAKES: *about 900g (2lb)*

2kg (4½lb) ripe plum tomatoes
2 tsp caster sugar
1 tbsp oregano or marjoram
  leaves, plus extra sprigs
1 tsp salt
good-quality extra virgin olive
  oil, for covering

The long, slow cooking at a low temperature draws out the natural sweetness of the humble plum tomato, creating a delicious and intense flavour that you can enjoy year round.

1 Set wire racks over lipped baking sheets (cookie sheets). Halve the tomatoes and arrange closely together on the racks, cut side down. Leave to drain for 30 minutes.

2 Preheat the oven to the lowest temperature setting you can – I've used 80°C/175°F/gas mark ¼.

3 Turn the tomatoes over and sprinkle with the sugar, herbs and salt.

4 Put the tomatoes in the oven and wedge a skewer in the door to keep it slightly ajar. Cook for 8–10 hours until dried out – this is a matter of preference. I prefer a softer sunblush texture and flavour while others like to dry them out completely. It's up to you.

5 Pack into sterilised jars and submerge entirely with olive oil. Add a sprig of fresh oregano or marjoram, if you like, then seal. These tomatoes keep for up to a year unopened. Once opened, store in the fridge and use within two weeks. And the bonus is that you can use the tomato-infused oil for dressings or cooking.

PICKLED CHERRIES

PREPARATION: *25 minutes,*
 plus standing
COOKING: *7 minutes*
MAKES: *about 1.2kg (2½lb)*

1kg (2¼lb) cherries (I use
 Morello but Duke or Royal
 varieties work well too)
500g (1lb 2oz) granulated sugar
400ml (13½fl oz) distilled white
 vinegar
2cm (¾in) piece root ginger,
 sliced
6 cloves
1 cinnamon stick, broken in half

With all manner of uses, make these cherries for yourself or a friend who
hankers after a sweet and sour cocktail, as a grown-up accompaniment
to roast meats, especially pork and game, or to serve with cheese.

1 Prepare the cherries. Whether you stone the cherries or not is up to
you; I prefer to keep them in as the stones impart a pleasing, subtle
almond flavour. I also keep the stalks intact because they look prettier
on the plate. If you decide to keep the stones, pierce each cherry two or
three times with a skewer.
2 Put all the remaining ingredients, except the cherries, in a deep pan
and heat gently to dissolve the sugar.
3 Add the cherries to the pan, cover and poach for about 5–7 minutes
until just tender. Using a slotted spoon, transfer the cherries to hot
sterilised jars, leaving a 1cm (½in) gap at the top.
4 Cover the fruit with the poaching syrup, tucking the ginger and
cinnamon pieces into the jars too and seal. Leave in a cool, dark place
for a month before giving away or eating.

A wonderful spread of jars. Here we have a mixture of *Fruits of the forest conserve* and *Apricot and amaretto jam*.

APRICOT AND AMARETTO JAM

PREPARATION: *35 minutes,*
plus standing
COOKING: *about 25 minutes*
MAKES: *about 1.2kg (2½lb)*

1kg (2¼lb) ripe apricots
1kg (2¼lb) granulated sugar
juice of 1 lemon
300ml (10fl oz) water
2 tbsp amaretto

Apricots have a natural affinity with almonds. In this jam, I enhance this by extracting the pleasing almond flavour of the apricot kernels and by adding some amaretto liqueur.

1 Halve the apricots and remove the stones. Set the stones aside. Quarter or roughly chop the apricots, depending on how chunky you like your jam to be.

2 Crack open the apricot stones with a pair of nutcrackers. Remove the kernels and discard the shells. Bring a pan of water to the boil, add the apricots kernels and boil for 2 minutes. Drain.

3 Put two or three saucers in the freezer, so they're really cold and ready to use to test for a set later on.

4 Put the apricots, blanched kernels and lemon juice into a preserving pan along with the water. Simmer gently for 5–10 minutes until the fruit is tender – this time will depend on their ripeness.

5 Add the sugar and heat gently until dissolved – it's important to make sure all the crystals are dissolved.

6 Bring to the boil and boil for 10–15 minutes; stir from time to time as this jam can catch on the base of the pan. After 10 minutes, test for the setting point: put a teaspoon of the jam on one of the freezing-cold saucers (take the pan off the heat while you do this). Leave for 1–2 minutes then push the jam with your finger – when it's ready, it should wrinkle. If it fails to wrinkle, continue boiling and test for a set every 5 minutes. (If you're using a sugar thermometer, the setting temperature is 104°C/220°F.)

7 Turn off the heat and leave to stand for 15 minutes. Skim off any scum, ladle the jam into hot sterilised jars and cover the surface with discs of waxed paper (the waxy side should be jam side down) and seal. Label the jars when completely cold. This jam keeps for up to a year unopened. Once opened, use within two months.

FRUITS OF THE FOREST CONSERVE

PREPARATION: **15 minutes**
COOKING: **20 minutes**
MAKES: **about 1.2kg (2½lb)**

1kg (2¼lb) mixed summer
  berries, such as raspberries,
  blackberries, tayberries,
  loganberries or blueberries
1kg (2¼lb) granulated or
  preserving sugar
200ml (7fl oz) water
juice of 2 lemons

Whatever berries you can get your hands on – from the garden or local hedgerows – will be transformed into this beautifully coloured and wonderfully tasty jam. Make sure that your mix of fruit contains a high proportion of high-pectin berries (such as raspberries, redcurrants and blackcurrants) to ensure a good set.

1 Two days before you plan to make the conserve, put the fruit and sugar in a large bowl, stir carefully, cover with clingfilm (plastic wrap) and leave to macerate at room temperature. The sugar will mingle with the fruit and draw out their natural juices.

2 Put two or three saucers in the freezer, so they're really cold and ready to use to test for a set later on.

3 Put the berries and sugar in a preserving pan with the water and the lemon juice. Heat gently to dissolve the sugar – it's important to make sure all the crystals are melted.

4 Bring to the boil and boil for 10–15 minutes. After 10 minutes, test for the setting point: put a teaspoon of the jam on one of the freezing-cold saucers (take the pan off the heat while you do this). Leave for 1–2 minutes then push the jam with your finger – when it's ready, it should wrinkle. If it fails to wrinkle, continue boiling and test for a set every 5 minutes. (If you're using a sugar thermometer, the setting temperature is 104°C/220°F.)

5 Turn off the heat and leave to stand for 15 minutes. Skim off any scum, ladle the jam into hot sterilised jars and cover the surface with discs of waxed paper (the waxy side should be jam side down) and seal. Label the jars when completely cold. This jam keeps for up to a year unopened. Once open, use within two months.

Even the simplest jar can be used and transformed with a fabric or paper top.

Capture ripe peaches in a heady syrup for a serving of summertime, whatever the time of year. These peaches taste great served with ice cream and crêpes – why not enjoy a small glass of the peach-flavoured liqueur alongside?

BOURBON PEACHES

PREPARATION: **15 minutes,**
 plus standing
COOKING: **2 minutes**
MAKES: **about 1.8kg (4lb)**

1 vanilla pod, split
400g (14oz) granulated sugar
900ml (1 pint 10½fl oz) water
6–8 ripe peaches, halved and
 stoned
300ml (10fl oz) Bourbon whiskey

1 Put the vanilla pod, sugar and water into a large pan and heat gently until the sugar has dissolved. Turn up the heat and boil for 2 minutes, then set aside to cool.
2 Pierce each peach several times with a skewer. Pack into a sterilised jar.
3 Stir the Bourbon into the sugar syrup and pour over the peaches, making sure they are submerged entirely. Seal and leave to stand in a cool, dark place for two months before eating. These peaches keep indefinitely if unopened. Once opened, eat within one month.

STRAWBERRY PASTILLES

PREPARATION: *30 minutes*
COOKING: *30–45 minutes*
MAKES: *about 650g (1lb 7oz)*

500g (1lb 2oz) strawberries, hulled
500g (1lb 2oz) preserving sugar
juice of ½ lemon
caster (superfine) sugar, for sprinkling

Take full advantage of any glut of strawberries, either from your garden or a trip to a local pick-your-own farm, and transform this summery fruit into chewy, luscious jellies, which will lengthen the time you can enjoy the wonderful taste of these delicious berries.

1 Dampen a 30cm x 26cm (12in x 10¼in) tin with water and line with clingfilm (plastic wrap).
2 Put the strawberries in a food processor and purée till smooth.
3 Put this purée, along with the sugar and lemon juice into a non-stick pan and heat gently to dissolve the sugar. Bring to the boil and cook steadily, stirring constantly until the purée is very thick – it'll take about 15 minutes. Pay close attention, as once the mixture starts to thicken it is prone to catching on the bottom of the pan.
4 Next, pour into the prepared tin, spread out evenly with the back of a spoon and leave to set overnight in a cool place.
5 Turn out onto a chopping board and cut into squares (I make mine about 2cm (¾in) square or use a small heart cutter, as shown here). Sprinkle plenty of caster (superfine) sugar onto a sheet of baking parchment and roll the jelly cubes in the sugar to coat. These pastilles keep for four weeks in an airtight container or sealed packet.

The delights of chocolate

MENDIANTS

PREPARATION: *20 minutes,*
  plus setting
COOKING: **5 minutes**
MAKES: *about 25*

100g (3½oz) dark, milk or white
  chocolate, broken into pieces

TO DECORATE:
raisins
crystallised violets or roses
strips of dried figs
candied peel
pistachio nuts
coloured sprinkles

Make these sophisticated chocolate buttons with your favourite type of chocolate – whether it's white, milk or dark – or, even better, a special selection of all three types.

1 Draw 25 3.5cm (1½in) circles on a large piece of silicone paper (or baking parchment) with a black marker pen. Turn the paper over and put on to a worktop or marble slab – ideally choose somewhere you can leave the buttons to cool without moving them as they will take a couple of hours to set.

2 Put two-thirds of the chocolate into a heatproof bowl set over a pan of gently simmering water. Once the chocolate is melted and has reached 45°C (113°F), stir in the remaining chocolate. The temperature should drop and once it is at 30°C (86°F) it is ready to use. This two-step melting is a simple form of tempering, which keeps the chocolate looking glossy. However, if you don't mind losing the glossiness of the chocolate, you can melt it all at once and continue the recipe.

3 Using a teaspoon, drizzle a little of the chocolate on to a circle and spread into a button shape. Only shape five or six at a time, keeping the rest of the chocolate over the hot water.

4 Garnish each button with your chosen decorations, then continue in batches with the rest of the chocolate. Leave to set completely before peeling them off the paper and packing into cellophane bags or jars. Don't chill them as the chocolate will lose its lovely glossiness.

WHITE CHOCOLATE AND ROSEMARY TRUFFLES

These rich and interesting truffles offer a delicate balance of white chocolate with aromatic rosemary. I find that the rosemary tempers the sweetness of the white chocolate so it doesn't end up too sickly. See what you think.

PREPARATION: **40 minutes**
COOKING: **5 minutes**
MAKES: *about 30*

100ml (3½fl oz) *double cream*
a large sprig rosemary
200g (7oz) *white chocolate,*
  broken into pieces
1 tbsp *liquid glucose*
25g (1oz) *unsalted butter*
sunflower oil, for greasing
icing sugar, for dusting

1 Put the cream and rosemary in a small pan and bring to the boil – this is important, otherwise the ganache won't thicken when whisked. Put the chocolate into a heatproof bowl. Pour over the cream and rosemary and stir once or twice.

2 Set the bowl over a pan of very gently simmering water, add the liquid glucose and butter. Leave to melt, stirring once or twice to combine. Set aside until cooled to room temperature. Lightly oil a disposable foil container 18cm x 13cm (7in x 5in).

3 Discard the rosemary. When cool, beat the mixture with electric beaters until soft, fluffy and paler in colour. Pour into the oiled container and put into the fridge to set.

4 Lay out a large piece of baking parchment on your worktop and dust liberally with icing sugar.

5 Retrieve the foil container from the fridge and snip its edges so that you can carefully peel them away. Turn out the truffle block onto a board. Cut into 3cm (1¼in) cubes (you'll need to clean the knife with kitchen paper every few cuts) and transfer the truffles to the icing-sugar-covered baking parchment as you go.

6 Dust the truffle cubes with more icing sugar and roll, pressing gently, to cover them completely.

7 Transfer the truffles to petit-four cases and arrange in lidded boxes. Store in the fridge, where they can be kept for up to two weeks.

HAZELNUT TRUFFLES

PREPARATION: *40 minutes,*
  plus chilling
COOKING: *5 minutes*
MAKES: *about 35*

120ml (4fl oz) double cream
120g (4oz) milk chocolate,
  broken into pieces
120g (4oz) chocolate hazelnut
  spread
1 tbsp liquid glucose
50g (1¾oz) unsalted butter
sunflower oil, for greasing
150g (5½oz) hazelnuts, toasted
  and finely chopped

I love making truffles, but my least favourite part is rolling them into balls as I tend to get covered in melted chocolate. Instead, I pour the mixture into a tray and cut them into squares once set. It's much quicker and these cubic delights look pleasingly different to the usual shapes.

1 Bring the cream to the boil in a small pan – this is important, otherwise the ganache won't thicken when whisked. Put the chocolate into a heatproof bowl. Pour over the cream and stir once or twice.
2 Set the bowl over a pan of very gently simmering water, add the spread, liquid glucose and butter. Leave to melt, stirring once or twice to combine. Set aside until cooled to room temperature. Lightly oil a disposable foil container 18cm x 13cm (7in x 5in).
3 When cool, beat the mixture with electric beaters until soft, fluffy and paler in colour. Pour into the container and put into the fridge to set.
4 Lay out a large piece of baking parchment on your worktop and spread half of the chopped hazelnuts onto it.
5 Retrieve the foil container from the fridge and snip its edges so that you can carefully peel them away. Turn out the truffle block onto a board. Cut into 3cm (1¼in) cubes (you'll need to clean the knife with kitchen paper every few cuts) and transfer the truffles to the nut-covered baking parchment as you go.
6 Sprinkle the remaining hazelnuts over the truffle cubes and roll, pressing gently, to cover them completely in the nuts.
7 Transfer the truffles to petit-four cases and arrange in lidded boxes. Store in the fridge, where they can be kept for up to two weeks.

WHISKY AND GINGER TRUFFLES

PREPARATION: *40 minutes,*
   plus chilling
COOKING: **5 minutes**
MAKES: *about 35–40*

150ml (5fl oz) *double cream*
250g (9oz) *dark chocolate,*
   broken into pieces
3 balls stem ginger, diced, and
   1 tbsp of the syrup
1 tbsp golden syrup
50g (1¾oz) *unsalted butter*
sunflower oil, for greasing
2 tbsp whisky
cocoa powder, for dusting

With a rich and intense flavour, these truffles are truly divine. This truffle mixture works well with most liqueurs, especially brandy, amaretto and cointreau; though do omit the ginger and syrup if you're varying flavours.

1 Put the cream in a small pan and bring to the boil – this is important, otherwise the ganache won't thicken when whisked. Put the chocolate into a heatproof bowl. Pour in the cream and stir once or twice.
2 Set the bowl over a pan of gently simmering water, add the ginger and syrup, golden syrup and butter. Leave to melt, stirring once or twice to combine. Set aside until cooled to room temperature. Lightly oil a disposable foil container 18cm x 13cm (7in x 5in).
3 When cool, beat the mixture with electric beaters until soft, fluffy and paler in colour. Beat in the whisky briefly. Pour into the oiled container and put into the fridge to set.
4 Lay out a large piece of baking parchment on your worktop and dust liberally with cocoa powder.
5 Retrieve the foil container from the fridge and snip its edges so that you can carefully peel them away. Turn out the truffle block onto a board. Cut into 3cm (1¼in) cubes (you'll need to clean the knife with kitchen paper every few cuts) and transfer the truffles to the cocoa-covered baking parchment as you go.
6 Dust the truffles with more cocoa powder and roll, pressing gently, to cover completely.
7 Transfer the truffles to petit-four cases and arrange in lidded boxes. Store in the fridge, where they can be kept for up to two weeks.

CHOCOLATE PEPPERMINT CRISP

PREPARATION: *20 minutes,*
plus setting
COOKING: *5 minutes*
MAKES: *250g (9oz)*

200g (7oz) dark chocolate,
broken into pieces
50g (1¾oz) crunchy demerara
sugar, plus extra for sprinkling
1½ tsp peppermint extract
sunflower oil, for greasing

Deliciously moreish, yet so simple to make, these after-dinner nibbles can be made in a variety of flavours, using other good-quality extracts, such as orange, cinnamon or coffee, as you wish.

1 Put the chocolate into a heatproof bowl set over a pan of gently simmering water. Leave to melt, stirring once or twice until smooth. Leave to cool slightly.
2 In a small bowl, mix together the sugar and peppermint extract. Stir into the cooled chocolate.
3 Pour onto a marble slab (or onto a lightly oiled baking sheet) and spread the chocolate out into a square about 23cm (9in) in size. Leave to set for a few minutes, then sprinkle over a spoonful of demerara sugar to decorate (if you do this too soon, the sugar will dissolve and the chocolate won't be crunchy).
4 When the chocolate has hardened, cut into randomly sized pieces. The peppermint crisp will keep for up to a month wrapped or in an airtight container, stored in a cool place.

Waxed paper parcels can be personalised with string and a label – simple but stylish.

TIFFIN

PREPARATION: *30 minutes,*
plus chilling
COOKING: *5 minutes*
MAKES: *36 squares*

150g (5½oz) unsalted butter
110g (3¾oz) golden syrup
1 tbsp brandy (optional)
60g (2oz) cocoa powder
200g (7oz) shortbread, roughly
    chopped
75g (2¾oz) raisins
75g (2¾oz) hazelnuts, toasted
300g (10½oz) milk chocolate,
    broken into pieces

A small piece of this nutty biscuity 'cake' delivers an intense chocolate hit, so you can cut it up into small pieces – perfect for serving as a petit four with an after-dinner coffee.

1 Line an 18cm (7in) square tin with baking parchment. Gently melt the butter and syrup in a pan, stirring to combine.
2 Put the remaining ingredients, except for the chocolate, into a bowl and mix well. Pour in the butter and syrup mixture and stir until thoroughly combined.
3 Pour into the prepared tin and level. Chill until solid.
4 Put the chocolate pieces into a heatproof bowl set over a pan of gently simmering water. Leave to melt, stirring once or twice until smooth. Pour evenly over the biscuit base and leave to set at room temperature.
5 Once set, cut into 2–3cm (¾–1¼in) squares. This tiffin keeps for up to two weeks in an airtight container or sealed packet.

PANFORTE

I like the diminutive version of this rich Italian confection and, of course, it means you'll have more to give away. You can, if you prefer, make a larger version (using a 21cm (8in) tin) and cut into wedges before wrapping; if you do, you'll need to increase the baking time to 1 hour.

PREPARATION: **45 minutes**
COOKING: **1 hour**
MAKES: **4 cakes of 10cm (4in)**

150g (5½oz) each of pistachios
    and hazelnuts
vegetable oil, for greasing
275g (9¾oz) candied peel
½ tsp ground cinnamon
¼ tsp each of ground allspice,
    nutmeg, coriander and white
    pepper
50g (1¾oz) plain flour
25g (1oz) cocoa powder
110g (3¾oz) granulated sugar
175g (6¼oz) clear honey
icing sugar, for dredging

1 Preheat the oven to 180°C/350°F/gas mark 4, and have a couple of dessertspoons and a mug of hot water handy.
2 Spread the nuts onto a baking sheet and bake for 10 minutes until lightly golden. Remove from the oven, cool, then roughly chop.
3 Lower the temperature to 150°C/300°F/gas mark 2. Grease and line the bases of four 10cm (4in) springform cake tins with baking parchment.
4 Put the peel, spices, flour and cocoa into a large bowl along with the nuts. Stir to combine. Keep warm while you make the sugar syrup.
5 Heat the sugar and honey gently in a small pan until the sugar has dissolved. Then bring to the boil and cook until it reaches 121°C/250°F (the hard ball stage) on a sugar thermometer. If you don't have a thermometer, drop a teaspoon of the mixture into a bowl of cold water. Bring it together with your fingers – it should form a hard ball.
6 Working quickly, stir the sugar syrup into the flour mixture. Wet a couple of dessertspoons and use them to transfer the mixture into the cake tins. Press down firmly. Be patient – the mixture is sticky.
7 Bake the panforte in a preheated oven for 35–40 minutes.
8 Remove from the oven and cool on a wire rack. Slide a knife around the edges to loosen. Remove from the tins, peel away the parchment and dredge the tops of the panforte with icing sugar. I find it's best wrapped in cellophane. This panforte keeps for up to two months when wrapped or stored in an airtight container.

CHOCOLATE KISSES

PREPARATION: *40 minutes,*
   plus chilling
COOKING: *10 minutes*
MAKES: **16**

100g (3½oz) milk chocolate,
   broken into pieces
100g (3½oz) dark chocolate,
   broken into pieces
25g (1oz) butter
5 tbsp double cream
1 tsp rosewater
1 tsp violet liqueur
crystallised rose petals and
   violets, to decorate

The most English of chocolates, but never out of fashion, floral creams are just dreamy. These are my twist on the classic rose and violet creams that my grandmother adored.

1 Arrange 16 foil petit-four cases on a tray or baking sheet. Melt the milk chocolate in a heatproof bowl set over a pan of gently simmering water, stirring once or twice until smooth.

2 Spoon a little chocolate into each case and, using a small paint brush, paint the insides of the case. Leave to set in the fridge.

3 Repeat step 2 twice more and then leave to set completely, preferably overnight. Then, very carefully peel away the foil cases.

4 Put the dark chocolate and butter into a bowl. Heat the cream in a small pan and bring to the boil, then pour over the chocolate and butter. Set this bowl over a pan of gently simmering water and stir once or twice until the chocolate has completely melted. Set aside until cooled to room temperature.

5 Beat the chocolate mixture until light and fluffy. Divide into two and add the rosewater to one half and the violet liqueur to the other.

6 Fill a piping bag fitted with a star nozzle and pipe a swirl of the chocolate rose mixture into half of the chocolate cases. Top with a crystallised rose petal. Repeat with the violet mixture and top with a crystallised violet.

7 Transfer the chocolates into new cases. These chocolates keep for up to a week chilled but they're best enjoyed at room temperature.

RIGHT *A delightful selection of Chocolate kisses with crystallised rose and violet petals and Salted caramel cups. Coffee anyone?*

SALTED CARAMEL CUPS

PREPARATION: *50 minutes,*
 plus chilling
COOKING: *20 minutes*
MAKES: *16*

175g (6¼oz) dark chocolate,
 broken into pieces
60g (2oz) caster sugar
1 tbsp water
40ml (1½fl oz) double cream
15g (½ oz) unsalted butter
¼–½ tsp salt
gold edible sprinkles, to decorate
 (optional)

The dreamy combination of salt and sweet is hard to beat. Here I pair the two in dainty cases. They're the perfect size to pop in your mouth.

1 Arrange 16 foil petit-four cases on a tray or baking sheet. Melt 100g (3½oz) of the chocolate in a heatproof bowl set over a pan of gently simmering water, stirring once or twice until smooth.
2 Spoon a little chocolate into each case and, using a small paint brush, paint the insides of the case. Leave to set in the fridge.
3 Repeat step 2 twice more and then leave to set completely, preferably overnight. Then, very carefully peel away the paper cases.
4 Heat the sugar and water in a small deep pan until the sugar has dissolved. Brush the sides with a wet pastry brush to dissolve any stray sugar crystals. Boil for 5–6 minutes until the syrup is deep amber.
5 Remove from the heat and stir in the cream – be aware that it will bubble up, but keep stirring. Stir in the butter and salt. Set the caramel aside to cool to room temperature.
6 Fill the cases with the caramel. Chill until firm.
7 Melt the remaining chocolate as in step 1. Smooth a layer of chocolate across the caramel to seal. Sprinkle with the gold decorations and chill.
8 Transfer the chocolates into clean petit-four cases. These caramel cups keep for up to a week chilled but they're best savoured served at room temperature.

*Create a selection of chocolates
and truffles for a favourite
chocoholic friend.*

CHOCOLATE FUDGE SAUCE

PREPARATION: *20 minutes*
COOKING: *about 10 minutes*
MAKES: *about 550g (1lb 3½oz)*

300ml (10fl oz) double cream
100g (3½oz) light muscovado
   sugar
2 tbsp golden syrup
25g (1oz) unsalted butter
200g (7oz) dark chocolate,
   broken into pieces
1 tsp vanilla extract
a tiny pinch of salt

If you can stop yourself eating this rich and decadent chocolate sauce straight from the jar (it's hard, I can tell you!), then it's perfectly joyous melted and poured over ice cream.

1 Put the cream, sugar, syrup and butter into a pan. Heat gently, stirring, until the sugar has dissolved.

2 Bring to the boil and bubble gently for 4 minutes until thickened. Remove from the heat, add the chocolate and stir until melted and thoroughly combined.

3 Stir in the vanilla and salt. Then, pour into sterilised containers, seal and label. This sauce keeps for up to two weeks in the fridge. To use, heat gently in a pan, stirring, until melted.

A savoury
treat

SMOKY NUTS

PREPARATION: *10 minutes*
COOKING: *10 minutes*
MAKES: *300g (10½oz)*

300g (10½oz) mixed nuts, such
*   as cashews, blanched almonds,*
*   macadamias and brazil nuts*
1 tbsp olive oil
1 tsp sea salt
1 tsp smoked paprika

These nuts look fantastic packaged simply in cellophane or in a box divided into separate compartments. If you or a friend likes their nuts spicier, then simply add in a couple of pinches of chilli powder with the smoked paprika.

1 Preheat the oven to 180°C/350°F/gas mark 4.
2 Toss the nuts together or each type separately in the oil, depending on how you want to package them. Roast in a preheated oven for 5–10 minutes until golden.
3 Remove from the oven and then immediately toss in the salt and paprika and leave to cool.
4 These nuts keep for up to two weeks in an airtight container or sealed packet.

Package these in cellophane or a box divided into separate compartments.

SPICY SEEDS

PREPARATION: **5 minutes**
COOKING: **15 minutes**
MAKES: **about 320g (11¼oz)**

50g (1¾oz) sesame seeds
120g (4oz) sunflower seeds
120g (4oz) pumpkin seeds
1 tsp salt
½ tsp garam masala powder
1½ tbsp sunflower oil

These spicy seeds make an unusual and ever-so useful savoury gift to nibble on or sprinkle onto salads. You can vary the seed mix to match the preferences of the person you have in mind for the gift.

1 Preheat the oven to 200°C/400°F/gas mark 6 and line a baking sheet with baking parchment.
2 Meanwhile, mix together all of the ingredients until everything is coated well.
3 Tip them out and spread into one layer on the prepared baking sheet. Bake in a preheated oven for 10–15 minutes, turning once or twice, until golden.
4 Remove from the oven, leave to cool on the baking sheet and pack into sterilised jars. Seal the jars and label. These seeds keep for up to four weeks.

CHEESE STRAWS

PREPARATION: **15 minutes,**
 plus chilling
COOKING: **15 minutes**
MAKES: **12**

320g (11¼oz) ready-rolled
 puff pastry
milk, for brushing
6 tbsp Parmesan cheese, finely
 grated
sesame seeds and poppy seeds,
 for sprinkling (optional)

1 Preheat the oven to 220°C/425°F/gas mark 7, and line
two to three baking sheets with baking parchment.
2 Unroll the pastry sheet and trim the edges to neaten,
as necessary. Cut the pastry into four equal pieces, then
cut each quarter into strips 2cm (¾in) wide.
3 Brush each strip with milk and sprinkle with the cheese.
Give each strip a couple of twists, then arrange on the baking
sheets. If you like, sprinkle some of the straws with sesame or
poppy seeds. Chill for 20 minutes.
4 Bake the straws for 10–15 minutes until golden. Remove from
the oven and transfer to wire racks to cool. These cheese straws
keep for up to two weeks in an airtight container or sealed packet.

These moreish melt-in-the-
mouth morsels can be whipped
up in no time since they use
ready-rolled pastry. Why not
make some to take to a friend's
for dinner or package up as a
special savoury treat?

POPPY AND SESAME SEED CRACKERS

1 Sift the flour and baking powder into a bowl with the salt. Rub in the butter to give fine breadcrumbs; do this in a food processor, if you like.

2 Stir in the seeds. Sprinkle over the water and bring together the mixture with a flat-bladed knife to form a firm dough. Knead briefly until smooth. Flatten into a disc, wrap in clingfilm and chill for 20 minutes, so the dough will be firm enough to roll easily.

3 Meanwhile, preheat the oven to 180°C/350°F/gas mark 4, and lightly grease two or three baking sheets.

4 Roll out the dough on a lightly floured surface to a thickness of 3mm (⅛in). Stamp out squares with a 6cm (2½in) fluted cutter, cutting them close together and re-rolling any trimmings. Arrange on the baking sheets and prick all over with a fork.

5 Bake for 10–15 minutes until the edges are pale golden and crisp. If any of the biscuits puff up, push down gently with the back of a spoon.

6 Remove from the oven and cool on a wire rack. These biscuits keep for up to two weeks in an airtight container.

PREPARATION: **20 minutes, plus chilling**
COOKING: **15 minutes**
MAKES: **25–30**

250g (9oz) plain flour, plus extra
   for dusting
1 tsp baking powder
½ tsp salt
60g (2oz) unsalted butter, diced,
   plus extra for greasing
1 tbsp poppy seeds
1 tbsp sesame seeds
4–5 tbsp cold water

These make a perfect present for any fromageophiles in your life. Why not make up a mini hamper or basket with some fruit cheese (see page 80), pickled onions (see page 78) or a chutney (see page 74) for the ultimate cheeseboard accompaniment?

ROASTED BABY PEPPERS

PREPARATION: *35 minutes*
COOKING: *20 minutes*
MAKES: *about 750g (1lb 11¾oz)*

*500g (1lb 2oz) baby peppers (or
an equal weight of full-sized
peppers)*
1 tbsp white wine vinegar
2 sprigs thyme, leaves picked
1 tsp fennel seeds
extra virgin olive oil

These beautiful little peppers
liven up no end of dishes, from
salads to antipasti, or simply
serve as a predinner nibble.

1 Preheat the oven to 200°C/400°F/gas mark 6. Put the peppers in one layer in a roasting tray and roast for 20–25 minutes until lightly charred.
2 Immediately transfer the peppers to a large plastic bag and tie the ends together. Leave the peppers to sit in the bag for 10 minutes – the steam in the bag will loosen their skins.
3 When the peppers are cool enough to handle, peel away the skins. I try to keep the stalks intact as they look pretty when kept whole in the jar.
4 Put the peeled peppers in a large bowl with the vinegar, thyme and fennel seeds and any juices from the bag. Gently mix together.
5 Transfer to sterilised jars and cover the peppers completely with olive oil. Seal the jars and label. These peppers keep for up to three months. Once opened, chill and consume within two weeks.

SWEDISH CRISPBREADS

PREPARATION: *20 minutes,*
  plus rising
COOKING: *20 minutes*
MAKES: 20

250g (9oz) rye flour, plus extra
  for dusting
100g (3½oz) strong white bread
  flour
1 tsp easy fast-action yeast
1 tbsp caraway seeds
½ tsp salt
200–250ml (7–8½fl oz) tepid
  water

To make authentic Swedish crispbreads, I use my knobbly Knäckebröd rolling pin, which is especially made for the job.

1 Put the flours, yeast, seeds and salt in a large bowl. Make a well in the centre and add enough of the water to make a firm dough.
2 Turn out onto a lightly floured work surface and knead for 10 minutes until smooth and elastic. Alternatively, use the dough hook on a free-standing mixer for 7 minutes. Cover and leave to rise for 45 minutes.
3 Divide the dough into 20 pieces and roll into balls. Meanwhile, preheat the oven to 230°C/455°F/gas mark 8.
4 Generously dust the work surface with rye flour and roll out each ball to a 11cm (4¼in) circle; if you don't have a Knäckebröd rolling pin and you're using a regular rolling pin, then simply prick all over with a fork.
5 Bake in a preheated oven in several batches for 2–5 minutes until brown and crisp. Remove from the oven and cool on wire rack. These crispbreads keep for up to two months in an airtight container.

A savoury treat   121

SWEET WHOLEMEAL BISCUITS

PREPARATION: *30 minutes,*
  plus chilling
COOKING: *20–25 minutes*
MAKES: *about 35*

425g (15oz) wholemeal flour
120g (4oz) fine oatmeal
1 tbsp baking powder
120g (4oz) golden caster sugar
180g (6½oz) butter, diced
150ml (5fl oz) milk

This most wonderfully versatile
biscuit can be enjoyed with a
cup of tea or with soft cheese as
part of a cheeseboard. So, from
a present-giving point of view,
it's an all-round winner.

1 Preheat the oven to 180°C/350°F/gas mark 4, and lightly grease two
or three baking sheets.
2 Put the flour, oatmeal, baking powder and sugar into a large mixing
bowl and rub in the butter until it resembles breadcrumbs – you could
do this in a food processor if you prefer.
3 Using a flat-bladed knife, add enough milk to the crumbs to make
a soft dough. Then, bring together with your hands and knead gently
until smooth. Shape into a disc, wrap in clingfilm and leave to rest for
20 minutes (put it in the fridge to rest if the kitchen is warm).
4 Roll out the dough on a lightly floured surface to a thickness of 5mm
(¼in). Cut out rounds with a 6–7cm (2½–2¾in) cutter, re-rolling any
trimmings. Arrange on the baking sheets and prick a few times with
a fork. Bake in a preheated oven for 20–25 minutes.
5 Remove from the oven and cool for a couple of minutes on the trays
before transferring to wire racks to cool. These biscuits keep for up to
a month in an airtight container or sealed packet.

BLUE CHEESE AND SAGE MUFFINS

PREPARATION: *10 minutes*
COOKING: *20 minutes*
MAKES: 12

Make these muffins for the friend in your life who prefers savoury treats to sweet ones. For a milder flavour, I've found they also work well with a hard cheese, such as Cheddar.

225g (8oz) plain flour
225g (8oz) cornmeal (polenta)
2 tbsp baking powder
2 tbsp finely chopped sage leaves
½ tsp salt
4 medium eggs
400ml (13½fl oz) whole milk
50ml (2fl oz) sunflower oil
100g (3½oz) blue cheese,
  crumbled

1 Preheat the oven to 220°C/425°F/gas mark 7, and line a 12-hole muffin tray with paper cases.
2 Put the flour, cornmeal, baking powder, sage and salt into a large bowl. Make a well in the centre.
3 Beat together the eggs, milk and oil in a large jug. Pour this mixture into the dry ingredients and stir together until well combined. Lastly, stir in the cheese. It's quite a sloppy mix so don't panic.
4 Divide the muffin mixture between the paper cases and bake for 20–25 minutes until golden and risen. Remove from the oven and cool completely on a wire rack before wrapping. These muffins are best eaten within two days.

LEMON AND FENNEL OIL

PREPARATION: **10 minutes, plus standing**

MAKES: **600ml (1 pint)**

600ml (1 pint) good-quality extra virgin olive oil

1 tsp fennel seeds, lightly crushed

finely grated zest of 1 unwaxed lemon

fennel herb sprig, to finish (optional)

wide strip of lemon peel, to finish (optional)

1 Put the ingredients into a large jar or bowl. Cover with a lid or clingfilm and leave in a cool, dark place for a month, swirling occasionally.

2 Strain the oil into sterilised bottles. Add a sprig of fresh fennel herb and a strip of lemon peel to each bottle, if you like. Seal and label. Store in a cool, dry place out of sunlight for up to six months.

This wonderfully aromatic oil has myriad uses, but I like to use it in salad dressings or in a marinade for fish or poultry.

MARINATED OLIVES

PREPARATION: *20 minutes, plus marinating*
MAKES: *about 200g (7oz) of each flavour*

600g (1lb 5oz) green or black olives or a mixture of both, drained
360ml (12fl oz) olive oil
150ml (5fl oz) white wine vinegar
12 garlic cloves, sliced thinly

If I'm invited to friends for supper, I like to take along a pot of these marinated olives as a gift for the host – it makes a welcome change from flowers or chocolates.

1 Divide the olives between three non-metallic bowls. Divide the oil, vinegar and garlic between each set of olives.
2 Stir in each flavouring. Cover and leave to marinate overnight.
3 Decant into sterilised jars, seal and label. Keep chilled and use any of these marinated olives within two weeks.

FOR GREEK OLIVES:
2 sprigs each oregano and thyme
2 slices lemon, cut into small wedges

FOR ITALIAN OLIVES:
2 sprigs rosemary
1 tsp fennel seeds
1 tsp mixed peppercorns

FOR MIDDLE EASTERN OLIVES:
1 tsp each cumin and coriander seeds
finely grated zest of 1 lemon and 1 orange

MARINATED GOAT'S CHEESE

PREPARATION: *20 minutes*
MAKES: *about 500g (1lb 2oz)*

300g (10½oz) goat's cheese,
  cubed
75g (2¾oz) green olives
thyme or rosemary sprigs
fresh bay leaves
few wide strips of lemon zest
extra virgin olive oil

Transform shop-bought goat's cheese into something truly special.
It's delicious eaten on its own but can enliven any salad or pizza and
equally sits right at home in a platter of antipasti. I've found this recipe
also works well with feta.

1 Fill sterilised jars two-thirds full with the goat's cheese and olives.
Tuck in a herb sprig, bay leaf and piece of lemon zest.
2 Top up with the olive oil, making sure the cheese and olives are
covered. Seal and label. Chill and eat within two weeks.

ROSEMARY GRISSINI

PREPARATION: *30 minutes,*
  plus rising
COOKING: *15 minutes*
MAKES: 24

400g (14oz) strong white flour
2 tbsp finely chopped rosemary
½ tsp salt
1 tsp fast-action dried yeast
3 tbsp olive oil, plus extra for
  greasing and brushing
220ml (7½fl oz) tepid water

Breadsticks – or as the Italians say 'grissini' – are hard to beat for nibbling or dipping, and home-made ones, with their lovely 'each one is slightly different' appeal, make great gifts. Partner them with one or more of the items in my Italian kit (see page 165).

1 Put the flour, rosemary and salt into a large bowl and stir in the yeast. Make a well in the centre and pour in the olive oil and enough warm water to make a soft but not too sticky dough.
2 Lightly flour a work surface and knead the dough for 10 minutes until smooth and elastic. Transfer the dough into a lightly oiled bowl, cover with a tea towel and leave to rise in a warm place for 1½ hours, until doubled in size.
3 Preheat the oven to 220°C/425°F/gas mark 7 and lightly oil two to three large baking sheets.
4 Divide the dough into 24 equal pieces (about 30g (1¼oz)) and roll each one under your fingers to form a long thin 'sausage' (about 30cm (12in) long). Arrange these 'sausages' spaced apart on the baking sheets and brush with some oil.
5 Bake in a preheated oven for 12–15 minutes until golden and hollow sounding. Remove from the oven and transfer to a wire rack to cool completely. These grissini keep for three days in an airtight container.

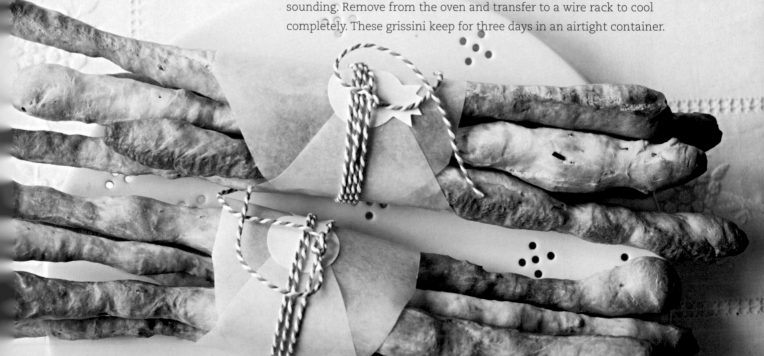

Raise a
glass

VANILLA CARAMEL LIQUEUR

PREPARATION: *15 minutes,*
  plus standing
MAKES: *about 750ml*
  (1 pint 6fl oz)

750ml (1 pint 6fl oz) vodka
150g (5½oz) soft vanilla caramel
  toffees

A gloriously sweet nectar that will tickle anyone's tastebuds. You can use the same method to flavour vodka with a variety of sweets, such as jelly beans or babies, Turkish delight or butterscotch. It's a perfect drink to personalise with someone's favourite sweeties.

1 Put the toffees into a wide-necked sealable jar. Pour over the vodka and allow the toffees to dissolve slowly. Seal the jar and store in a dark, cool place. Leave to infuse for a week, shaking every day to ensure the toffees are totally dissolved. (If you don't have the time, you can melt the toffees instead. Simply put the toffees in a heatproof bowl set over a pan of gently simmering water and leave to melt. Then, carefully transfer the liquid toffee into the jar and stir in the vodka. Seal and store as above.)

2 Decant the liqueur into sterilised bottles, seal and label. This bottle of loveliness keeps indefinitely. Shake well before using, as some toffees can cause it to separate on standing.

Decant into an unusual bottle, which can be reused and enjoyed again and again.

CRÈME DE CASSIS

PREPARATION: *15 minutes,*
 plus standing
MAKES: *about 1 litre (1¾ pints)*

500g (1lb 2oz) blackcurrants,
 de-stalked
2 whole cloves
1 small cinnamon stick
300g (10½oz) granulated sugar
750ml (1 pint 6fl oz) vodka or
 eau de vie

For an extra-special gift, pair this liqueur with a bottle of sparkling wine to make the classic Kir Royale.

1 Put the fruit and spices into a wide-necked sealable jar. Cover with the sugar, then pour over the vodka or eau de vie – by the way, the alcohol doesn't need to be expensive or top quality.
2 Seal the jar and store in a dark, cool place. Shake every day for the first week to dissolve the sugar, then just a couple of times a week. Leave to infuse for at least a month, but the longer you can bear to wait, the better it will taste.
3 Strain the fruit and liqueur through a muslin-lined sieve into a large jug. Decant the liqueur into sterilised bottles, seal and label. This liqueur keeps indefinitely, although it's unlikely to last long.

REDCURRANT GIN

PREPARATION: *15 minutes,
plus standing*
MAKES: *about 1 litre (1¾ pints)*

*350g (12oz) redcurrants, de-
stalked*
350g (12oz) granulated sugar
750ml (1 pint 6fl oz) gin

This glorious ruby-red liqueur is great whether drunk as a small measure or topped up with soda as a long drink. De-stalking currants can be fiddly and I find pulling a fork down the stem releases them nicely. But don't worry as you will be straining the liqueur after infusing.

1 Put the fruit into a wide-necked sealable jar. Cover with the sugar, then pour over the gin. By the way, the alcohol doesn't need to be expensive or top quality.
2 Seal the jar and store in a dark, cool place. Shake daily for the first week to dissolve the sugar, then twice a week. Leave to infuse for at least a month, but the longer you can wait the better it will taste.
3 Strain the fruit and liqueur through a muslin-lined sieve into a large jug. Decant the liqueur into sterilised bottles, seal and label. This liqueur keeps indefinitely. If you like, you can reward your efforts by eating the infused fruit, perhaps with a scoop of vanilla ice cream and a drizzle of the liqueur.

LEMON SCHNAPPS

Don't keep this citrussy liqueur just for sipping on its own; it tastes just wonderful when mixed with tonic for a long drink.

PREPARATION: *30 minutes*
MAKES: *about 1 litre (1¾ pints)*

6 large unwaxed lemons
750ml (1 pint 6fl oz) schnapps
250g (9oz) granulated sugar
200ml (7fl oz) water

1 Peel the rind away from the lemons with a vegetable peeler, making sure that you leave behind the bitter white pith.
2 Put the peel into a wide-necked sealable jar or bowl. Cover with the schnapps, seal or cover with clingfilm and leave in a cool, dark place for a week.
3 Heat the sugar and water gently in a pan to dissolve the sugar.
4 Strain the schnapps through a muslin-lined sieve, discarding the lemon peel. Stir in the sugar syrup.
5 Decant the liqueur into sterilised bottles, seal and label. Leave for at least two weeks before drinking, but the longer you leave it the better it tastes. This schnapps keeps indefinitely. I like to keep mine in the freezer.

COFFEE CREAM LIQUEUR

Serve this creamy, rich liqueur neat over ice or drizzle over ice cream for an indulgent after-dinner treat.

1 Put the coffee beans in a bowl, pour over the whisky, cover and leave to infuse overnight.

2 Heat the condensed milk and chocolate gently in a small pan, stirring once or twice, until the chocolate has melted.

3 Strain the whisky and put into a blender or food processor with the condensed milk and chocolate. Whizz for a minute or two to blend thoroughly and transfer to a bowl and chill overnight.

4 Remove any skin that might have formed during chilling and decant into sterilised bottles, seal and label. This superb tipple keeps for up to a month in the fridge.

PREPARATION: *30 minutes, plus infusing and chilling*
MAKES: *about 1 litre (1¾ pints)*

50g (1¾oz) *coffee beans*
550ml (19fl oz) *whisky*
397g (14oz) *canned sweetened condensed milk*
40g (1½oz) *dark chocolate, broken into pieces*

LE VIN D'ORANGE

This Provençal aperitif is traditionally made with Seville oranges. If you are making this when these wonderfully bitter oranges are in season, simply omit the lemon juice.

1 Blanch the whole oranges in boiling water for 3 minutes to kill off the natural yeasts on the surface that might cause fermentation. Drain.
2 Halve and squeeze the oranges. Put the juice and shells into a large bowl or sealable jar along with the remaining ingredients. Cover and leave to infuse for at least a month.
3 Strain through a muslin-lined sieve into a large jug. Decant into sterilised bottles, seal and label. This liqueur keeps indefinitely.

PREPARATION: *15 minutes,*
 plus standing
COOKING: *3 minutes*
MAKES: *about 1 litre (1¾ pints)*

3 large juicy oranges
juice 1 lemon
200g (7oz) granulated sugar
750ml (1 pint 6fl oz) rosé wine
150ml (5fl oz) vodka or eau
 de vie
1 vanilla pod, split and
 scraped

GOLDEN VODKA

PREPARATION: *20 minutes,*
  plus infusing
MAKES: *750ml (1 pint 6fl oz)*

2 vanilla pods, split
750ml (1 pint 6fl oz) vodka
2 sheets gold leaf (mine were
  5cm x 5cm (2in x 2in) each)

Who could fail to be impressed by this sumptuous golden vodka that reveals a special surprise when it's given a shake?

1 Pop the vanilla pods into the bottle of vodka and leave to infuse for at least a week. The vodka will steadily become a wondrous golden colour and will smell delightfully aromatic.
2 Remove the vanilla pods – you could wash and dry them and use to flavour some caster sugar if you like. Next, decant the vodka into your chosen sterilised gift bottles.
3 Gold leaf is incredibly delicate, so carefully pick up small flakes (do this on the paper it comes in) with a small, slightly damp paintbrush and drop into the bottle. (Don't worry if it blobs up as it gets wet because as soon as you drop it into the vodka it will expand into a flake again – watch it, it's magical!) Seal the bottles and label. This golden nectar keeps indefinitely.

Watch friends and family marvel at its magical appearance, with glittering gold flakes dancing around in the light.

ROSE AND LIME SYRUP

PREPARATION: *30 minutes*
COOKING: *10 minutes*
MAKES: *about 1.1 litres (1 pint 18½fl oz)*

1kg (2¼lb) granulated sugar
¼ tsp cream of tartar
1 vanilla pod, split
finely grated zest and juice of
   3 limes
1.2 litres (2 pints) water
2 tsp rosewater

A versatile syrup that can be used in cocktails, drizzled over pancakes or ice cream or simply diluted with sparkling water for a wonderfully refreshing summery drink.

1 Put the sugar, cream of tartar, vanilla pod and lime zest in a large pan with the water. Heat gently to dissolve the sugar then bring to the boil and bubble for 5 minutes until syrupy. Set aside to infuse for 30 minutes.
2 Strain the sugar syrup through a muslin-lined sieve. Stir in the lime juice and rosewater. Taste and add more rosewater if necessary.
3 Decant into sterilised bottles, seal and label. This syrup keeps for four weeks in the fridge.

RHUBARB AND GINGER CORDIAL

PREPARATION: *25 minutes*
COOKING: *15 minutes*
MAKES: *about 1 litre (1¾ pints)*

1kg (2¼lb) rhubarb, chopped
40g (1½oz) root ginger, grated
1 star anise
1 litre (1¾ pints) water
granulated sugar
2 tsp citric acid

This refreshing cordial has the most glorious pink colour – search out the pinkest rhubarb. As well as drinking diluted with water (fizzy or still), I like to make a rhubarb Bellini (mix 1 part cordial to 5 parts Prosecco).

1 Put the rhubarb, ginger and star anise in a large pan with the water. Bring to the boil, then simmer for 10 minutes until the rhubarb is tender.
2 Set a sieve over a large bowl and pour in the rhubarb and juice – you'll need to do this in batches. Push down on the fruit with the back of a spoon to extract as much juice as you can. (Don't throw away the rhubarb flesh – you can sweeten it and eat with yogurt.)
3 Now, measure the volume of juice you have – you will need 350g (12oz) granulated sugar for every 500ml (18fl oz) of liquid. Put the juice and sugar into a pan set over a low heat until the sugar has dissolved, then stir in the citric acid.
4 Strain the cordial through a muslin-lined funnel into sterilised bottles. Seal and label. The cordial keeps for up to a year unopened. Once opened, store it in the fridge and use within two weeks.

small but
perfectly formed

MINI CHRISTMAS CAKES

PREPARATION: 45 minutes,
  plus macerating
COOKING: 4½ hours
MAKES: 9

340g (11¾oz) currants
200g (7oz) each of sultanas and
  raisins
120g (4oz) dried figs, diced
zest and juice of 1 lemon
3½ tbsp chocolate-based liqueur
  or brandy
300g (10½oz) unsalted butter,
  soft plus extra for greasing
75g (2¾oz) candied peel
75g (2¾oz) macadamia nuts,
  chopped
75g (2¾oz) dark chocolate drops
300g (10½oz) dark muscovado
  sugar
1 tbsp black treacle
5 medium eggs, lightly beaten
300g (10½oz) plain flour
1 tsp mixed spice
4–6 tbsp brandy, for feeding

TO DECORATE:
500g (1lb 2oz) golden marzipan
110g (3¾oz) apricot jam, plus
  1 tbsp water
1kg (2¼lb) ready-to-roll fondant
  icing
icing sugar, for dusting
edible glitter, for dusting

1 Put the currants, sultanas, raisins, figs, lemon zest and juice and alcohol in a non-metallic bowl. Leave to macerate overnight.

2 Preheat the oven to 140°C/275°F/gas mark 1. Grease and double line the base and sides of a 23cm (9in) square cake tin with baking parchment. Wrap a double layer of brown paper around the tin and tie with string.

3 Stir the candied peel, nuts and chocolate chips into the fruity mixture.

4 Beat the butter and sugar with electric beaters for about 5 minutes until fluffy and much paler in colour. Then beat in the treacle.

5 Gradually beat in the eggs. If the mixture looks as if it's going to curdle, beat in 1 tablespoon of flour then carry on adding the eggs.

6 Using a large metal spoon, gently fold the flour and mixed spice into the mixture until well combined. Turn into the tin and smooth the top with the back of a spoon. Bake for 3–3½ hours until a skewer inserted comes out clean. Remove from the oven and cool in the tin set on a wire rack. Once the cake is cold, wrap tightly in baking parchment and a layer of foil. Store in a cool, dry place, feeding it weekly with 1 tbsp brandy.

7 A few days before you plan to give the cakes, you will need to cover the tops with a layer of marzipan. First unwrap the cake and cut into 9 equal squares. Turn them over so that the more level bottoms become the tops. Roll out the marzipan to a 5mm (¼in) thickness and cut out 9 squares the same size as the cake.

8 Melt the jam with the water then sieve to remove any lumps. Brush the tops of the cake with the jam. Brush away any crumbs and fix the marzipan on top. Leave in a cool place to dry out for two days.

9 When you're ready to decorate, dust a work surface with icing sugar and roll out the fondant icing to 5mm (¼in) thick. Brush the marzipan with water then place face down onto the icing. Carefully cut around the edges using the cake as a template. Turn the cake over and smooth the surface with the palm of your hand.

10 Stamp out Christmassy shapes with cutters and fix in place with a little water. Using a small paintbrush, dust some edible shimmer powder on top. Finish off with a ribbon and secure. Wrap in cellophane and tie with more ribbon. This cake keeps for up to two months.

My friends and family love these Christmas cakes in miniature. Sometimes, eating a full-sized version can seem overwhelming and can stretch on into the New Year, so my solution is to scale it down into a more manageable – and I have to say cute – size. You'll need to make the large cake at least four to six weeks before you divide it into smaller versions to decorate, because the flavour needs time to mature. Be warned, you will need a very large bowl to accommodate all the cake mixture – I have one that is brought out only once a year just for this job.

HAZELNUT BROWNIES

Anything in miniature is somehow irresistible and the same rings true for these nutty brownies. I dare you to find someone who could resist these rich, chocolately, nutty and squidgy squares.

PREPARATION: *35 minutes*
COOKING: *25 minutes*
MAKES: **28**

250g (9oz) butter, plus extra for greasing
250g (9oz) dark chocolate, broken into pieces
3 medium eggs, separated

225g (8oz) caster sugar
2 tbsp milk
2 tsp instant coffee dissolved in 1 tbsp boiling water
75g (2¾oz) self-raising flour
175g (6¼oz) hazelnuts, toasted and chopped
100g (3½oz) plain chocolate drops

1 Preheat the oven to 190°C/375°F/gas mark 5, and grease and line a 17cm x 30cm (6½in x 12in) baking tin with baking parchment.
2 Melt the chocolate pieces with the butter in a heatproof bowl set over gently simmering water. Cool slightly and meanwhile beat together the egg yolks, sugar, milk and coffee, and then the cooled chocolate. Fold in the flour using a metal spoon, followed by the nuts and chocolate drops.
3 In a separate bowl, whisk the egg whites until stiff and gently fold into the mixture. Carefully pour into the prepared tin and bake in a preheated oven for 20–25 minutes until just firm to the touch – a skewer inserted into the brownie should still have a little mixture clinging to it. You want the brownies to be squidgy, not dry.
4 Remove from the oven and leave to cool in the tin, then turn out and mark into squares when completely cold. Wrap in cellophane or store in an airtight container. These keep for up to two weeks.

MOCHA MUFFINS

A super-easy bake, muffins always meet with delighted faces when given as a gift. Here the coffee brings out the richness of the cocoa.

PREPARATION: *20 minutes*
COOKING: *15 minutes*
MAKES: 24

200g (7oz) caster sugar
350g (12oz) self-raising flour
50g (1¾oz) cocoa powder
2 tsp instant coffee dissolved in
  1 tbsp boiling water
250ml (8½fl oz) milk

120ml (4fl oz) sunflower oil
2 medium eggs, beaten

FOR THE ICING:
500g (1lb 2oz) icing sugar,
  sifted
2–3 tbsp hot water
few drops of coffee essence
chocolate coffee beans, to
  decorate (optional)

1 Preheat the oven to 200°C/400°F/gas mark 6, and line two 12-hole mini muffin trays with paper cases.
2 Sift the dry ingredients into a large bowl and make a well in the centre. In another bowl, add the milk and oil to the eggs and pour into the well. Quickly mix together and divide between the cases.
3 Bake in a preheated oven for 15 minutes, then remove from the oven and cool on a wire rack.
4 Mix together the icing sugar with the hot water and the coffee essence to make a spreadable icing. Decorate the muffins and top with a bean, if using. These muffins keep for two to three days in an airtight container or sealed packet.

MINI LEBKUCHEN

PREPARATION: *25 minutes,*
  plus cooling
COOKING: *12 minutes*
MAKES: 35–38

60g (2oz) butter
2 tbsp milk
250g (9oz) clear honey
225g (8oz) plain flour
2 tbsp cornflour
½ tsp each of ground coriander,
  ground ginger, ground
  cardamom (from about 6 pods)
  and ground cinnamon
1 tsp bicarbonate of soda

TO FINISH:
40g (1½oz) butter, melted
1 tbsp each caster sugar and
  icing sugar mixed together

Lebkuchen are a traditional baked Christmas treat in Germany; think of it a bit like gingerbread. I find the wonderful spice flavours improve with keeping, so make them at least a week before giving your gift.

1 Put the butter, milk and honey in a large pan and heat gently. Stir to combine and take off the heat.
2 Sift the flours, spices and bicarbonate of soda together in a bowl. Tip into the honey mixture and mix until smooth. Cover and leave to cool for a couple of hours.
3 Preheat the oven to 180°C/350°F/gas mark 4, and grease two or three baking sheets.
4 Take teaspoon heaps of the mixture and roll into walnut-sized balls. Arrange on the baking sheets, spaced well apart.
5 Bake in a preheated oven for 10–12 minutes.
6 Remove from the oven, allow to cool for a minute or so and then brush each biscuit with melted butter and dust with the sugar mix. Cool completely on a wire rack. These biscuits keep for a month in an airtight container or sealed packet.

FLORENTINES

PREPARATION: **25 minutes**
COOKING: **40 minutes**
MAKES: **28–30**

60g (2oz) butter, plus extra for
  greasing
50g (1¾oz) golden caster sugar
2 tbsp double cream
25g (1oz) cranberries
40g (1½oz) flaked almonds,
  roughly chopped
25g (1oz) mixed candied peel
25g (1oz) stem ginger, chopped
25g (1oz) pine nuts
15g (½oz) plain flour
50g (1¾oz) dark chocolate,
  melted, to finish

These rich, Italian-style biscuits are perfect with a cup of after-dinner coffee. Pine nuts aren't traditional but I find they add a pleasing crunch.

1 Preheat the oven to 180°C/350°F/gas mark 4, and grease two to three baking sheets.
2 Put the butter and sugar into a pan and heat gently to dissolve the sugar. Bring to the boil and, off the heat, add the cream.
3 Beat in the rest of the ingredients. Put ½ teaspoon heaps of the mixture on the baking sheets, spacing them well apart. Bake in batches, as you will need to work quickly when they come out of the oven.
4 Bake in a preheated oven for 8 minutes, then using a metal, round 5–6cm (2–2½in) pastry cutter, quickly bring the edges of the spread biscuits to the centre to make a perfect round. Return to the oven for 2–3 minutes until a deep golden colour. Leave on the tray for 2–3 minutes until set, then transfer to a wire rack to cool.
5 When the biscuits are cold, spread the backs with a coating of melted chocolate, then mark into wavy lines with a fork. These chewy delights keep for up to two weeks in an airtight container or sealed packet.

LITTLE GEMS

PREPARATION: *45 minutes,*
plus resting
COOKING: *10–15 minutes*
MAKES: *about 80*

175g (6¼oz) plain flour
50g (1¾oz) icing sugar
100g (3½oz) butter, diced
1 medium egg
1 tsp vanilla extract
400g (14oz) royal icing
flavoured extracts, such as
orange, coffee and lemon
food colouring pastes

Transport yourself back to childhood with the sight of these super-cute and nostalgic iced biscuits in miniature.

1 Sift the flour into a bowl with the icing sugar. Rub in the butter to form breadcrumbs.
2 Stir in the egg and vanilla extract. Mix together with a flat-bladed knife until it clumps together. Bring together with your fingertips to form a very soft dough. Shape into a disc, wrap in clingfilm and chill for 1–2 hours until firm enough to roll. Meanwhile, preheat the oven to 190°C/375°F/gas mark 5, and lightly grease two or three baking sheets.
3 Unwrap the dough and roll out to a thickness of 5mm (¼in). Cut out bases with a 2.5cm (1in) flower-shaped cutter and arrange, spaced apart, on the baking sheets. Bake for 4–5 minutes until golden.
4 Remove from the oven and leave to cool on the baking sheets for a few minutes before transferring to a wire rack to cool.
5 Meanwhile, make up the royal icing according to the packet instructions. Divide into three or four separate bowls and flavour with your chosen extracts and corresponding food colourings. Fill a piping bag fitted with a fluted nozzle and pipe stars onto the cookies. Leave to set overnight. These little gems keep for up to a week in an airtight container or sealed packet.

MERINGUE MUSHROOMS

PREPARATION: *1 hour*
COOKING: *1 hour*
MAKES: *about 50*

4 medium egg whites, at room
* temperature*
225g (8oz) caster sugar
melted dark chocolate, to
* decorate*

I like to use these little meringue mushrooms to decorate my Bûche de Noël at Christmas time but they make cute edible gifts whatever the time of year.

1 Preheat the oven to 110°C/225°F/gas mark ¼, and line two baking sheets with baking parchment.
2 Whisk the egg whites until stiff but not dry. Whisk in the sugar 1 tablespoon at a time until the meringue is thick and glossy.
3 Fill a piping bag fitted with a large plain nozzle and pipe 3.5cm (1½in) dome shapes on to the baking sheets, spaced apart. Vertically pipe stem shapes alongside about 3cm (1¼in) high. Bake in a preheated oven for about 45 minutes to 1 hour until they are completely dry and they easily lift away from the baking parchment.
4 To assemble, spread the underside of the mushroom cap with chocolate. Carefully make a hole in the centre with the tip of a skewer. Dip the pointed end of the stalk into the chocolate and carefully insert into the hole. Leave upside down until set (when the chocolate is almost set, score lines with a cocktail stick to represent the gills of the mushroom). These cute meringue shapes keep for two weeks in an airtight container or sealed packet.

LEMON SYRUP LOAF CAKES

PREPARATION: *35 minutes*
COOKING: *30 minutes*
MAKES: *8 mini loaves or a 900g*
   (2lb) loaf cake

175g (6¼oz) butter, very soft,
   plus extra for greasing
175g (6¼oz) self-raising flour
1 tsp baking powder
50g (1¾oz) fine polenta or
   cornmeal
finely grated zest of 1 lemon
175g (6¼oz) caster sugar
3 medium eggs, lightly beaten

FOR THE ICING:
50g (1¾oz) granulated sugar
juice of ½ lemon

Polenta adds a lovely crunchy texture to these mini loaves. If you can't find it in your local supermarket or deli, just increase the self-raising flour by the same amount instead.

1 Preheat the oven to 180°C/350°F/gas mark 4, and lightly grease and line the base and sides of eight 65ml (2½fl oz) mini loaf tins, or a 900g (2lb) loaf tin, with baking parchment; make sure the paper sits 1cm (½in) above the rim of the tins. Set the tins on a baking sheet.
2 Sift the flour and baking powder into a bowl. Stir in the polenta, then add the butter, lemon zest, sugar and eggs. Beat together for 2 minutes with electric beaters until fluffy and light in colour. Divide the mixture between the loaf tins and level the tops.
3 Bake in a preheated oven for 25–30 minutes (or 45 minutes–1 hour for the larger loaf cake) until risen and golden and a skewer inserted into the cakes comes out clean.
4 Remove from the oven and while the cakes are still hot, mix together the granulated sugar and lemon juice. Brush the tops of the cakes with the sugary mixture and leave to cool on a wire rack for 10 minutes. Remove from the tins and peel away the baking parchment. These little loaves keep for a week in an airtight container or wrapped in cellophane.

Gifts for
the cook

BRUNCH SET

A lovely little kit for a lazy weekend brunch. A tub of fresh blueberries, bottle of maple syrup and a packet of good coffee complete the gift.

FOR THE TROPICAL GRANOLA:

PREPARATION: **15 minutes**
COOKING: **20 minutes**
MAKES: **600g (1lb 5oz)**

250g (9oz) rolled porridge oats
150g (5½oz) flavoured clear
   honey (I like orange blossom
   honey)
1 tbsp sunflower oil
50g (1¾oz) coconut flakes
150g (5½oz) mixed chopped
   dried mango, pineapple and
   dates

1 Preheat the oven to 180°C/350°F/gas mark 4.
2 Put the oats into a large bowl. Then, put the honey and oil in a small pan and very gently warm it for a minute or two – this will make it easier to mix with the oats but be careful not to boil it.
3 Pour the honey mixture into the oats and mix thoroughly until all the ingredients are coated well.
4 Spread the granola out onto a large baking sheet. Bake for 10 minutes then stir in the coconut flakes and return to the oven for another 10 minutes until golden.
5 Remove from the oven and transfer to a bowl to cool. Then stir in the dried fruit. This granola keeps for up to a month when stored in an airtight container or a sealed packet.

FOR THE DRIED FRUIT COMPÔTE:

PREPARATION: **5 minutes**
COOKING: **15 minutes**
SERVES: **4–6**
500g (1lb 2oz) dried fruit, such
as apples, pears, apricots and
   prunes
1 cinnamon stick
½ tsp ground ginger
3 tbsp soft light brown sugar
330ml (11fl oz) apple juice

1 Put all of the ingredients into a pan and heat gently until the sugar has dissolved. Bring to the boil, then simmer for 10–15 minutes until syrupy.
2 Refrigerate overnight for the flavours to mingle and for the fruit to plump up. This compôte keeps for up to two weeks in the fridge. Serve at room temperature.

FOR THE PANCAKE MIX:
PREPARATION: **15 minutes**
MAKES: *about 15 pancakes*

120g (4oz) plain flour
1½ tsp baking powder
1 tbsp caster sugar
30g (1¼oz) sultanas

1 Mix together the dry ingredients and tip into a sterilised jar. Seal. Label and attach the recipe below.

To make the pancakes: Tip the pancake mix into a large bowl. Whisk in 1 medium egg and 300ml (10fl oz) milk until smooth. Put a greased non-stick frying pan over a medium heat. Pour in 2 tablespoons of batter. Cook for 4 minutes until the pancake bubbles, flip and cook for 3 minutes. Repeat with the remaining batter.

CHRISTMAS COOKIE KIT

1 Mix the flour with the baking powder, then tip into the jar. Shake gently to level out. Spoon in the sugar and roughly level out. Add the chocolate drops and the dried fruit.

2 Seal the jar and attach a biscuit cutter, wooden spoon and a hand-written label with the following recipe for these cookies.

CHERRY AND WHITE CHOCOLATE COOKIES

Melt 100g (3½oz) butter in a large pan with 120g (4oz) golden syrup. Add 1 large beaten egg, then stir in the cookie mixture. Mix to form a stiff dough. Divide into two pieces, flatten into discs and wrap in clingfilm. Chill for 20 minutes. Preheat the oven to 180°C/350°F/gas mark 4. Roll out the dough to a 3mm (⅛in) thickness, stamp out shapes with the cookie cutter; transfer to greased baking sheets. Make small holes in the top for threading cotton when baked, if you like. Bake in a preheated oven for 10–12 minutes until lightly golden. Cool on a wire rack; dust with icing sugar. Enjoy!

500g (1lb 2oz) plain flour
2 tsp baking powder
180g (6½oz) golden caster sugar
150g (5½oz) white chocolate drops
100g (3½oz) dried cranberries

PREPARATION:
15 minutes
MAKES: 25–30 cookies

I look out for pretty glass storage jars and wooden spoons at antique centres and charity shops. The jar needs to hold about 900g (2lb). Once the mixture has been turned into biscuits, they can be stored in the same jar, which is doubly pleasing.

GINGERBREAD HOUSE KIT

PREPARATION: *1½ hours*
COOKING: *10 minutes*
MAKES: *4 small houses*

350g (12oz) plain flour
1 tsp bicarbonate of soda
2 tbsp ground ginger
150g (5½oz) butter, diced
175g (6¼oz) light muscovado
  sugar
2 tbsp golden syrup, warmed
1 medium egg, beaten
4 x 250g (9oz) white royal icing
  sugar, for the 'glue'
assorted sweets, to decorate

Seek out a container that's roomy enough to fit all the elements of this super-sweet kit.

A ready-to-assemble gingerbread house is sure to be a big hit with adults and children alike. And with all the decorations and 'glue' supplied, there's no excuse not to get making it straight away.

1 Make templates from card using the measurements on page 172.
2 Put the flour, bicarbonate of soda, ginger and butter into a food processor. Whizz to form fine breadcrumbs, tip into a bowl and stir in the sugar.
3 Add the syrup and egg to the flour mixture and bring together with a flat-bladed knife until it forms clumps. Bring together with your hands to make a ball, then knead on a lightly floured work surface until smooth. Shape into a disc, wrap in clingfilm and chill for 20 minutes.
4 Divide the dough in half. Roll out the first half on a lightly floured surface to a thickness of 3mm (⅛in). Using the templates as a guide, cut out four of each shape, re-rolling the dough as necessary. Arrange on lightly greased baking sheets. Chill for 20 minutes.
5 Preheat the oven to 190°C/375°F/gas mark 5. Bake the gingerbread in a preheated oven for 8–10 minutes until golden. Neaten the edges while still warm, using the templates as a guide. Leave to set on the baking sheet for a few minutes then transfer to wire racks to cool. Keeps for up to three months.

To gift wrap: Line a box with waxed paper, put in the gingerbread shapes, interleaved with more waxed paper. Decant the royal icing sugar into cellophane packets; put the sweets into cellophane bags and tie with ribbon or colourful twine.

To assemble: First, prepare the 'glue' with the royal icing sugar and a few drops of water to make a mixture that's pipeable. Pipe a line of icing along the base of one of the side walls and fix upright onto a cake board. Pipe along the edge and base of a pointed end wall and fix to the side wall. Continue with the other side and end walls to form a box. Hold in place for a few minutes to allow the icing to set and glue the pieces together. Pipe icing along the top edges of the house and position the roof pieces in place. Decorate with the sweets, fixing in place with more icing. Use more icing to pipe windows and doors, if you like.

ITALIAN KIT

Everyone loves Italian food and this simple supper kit will go down a treat. Just add some good-quality pasta and a lump of Parmesan to finish off the gift.

FOR THE BASIL PESTO:
PREPARATION: *15 minutes*
MAKES: *about 350g (12oz)*

1 *small clove garlic*
100g (3½oz) *pine nuts toasted*
75g (2¾oz) *basil leaves*
100g (3½oz) *Parmesan, grated*
150–200ml (5–7fl oz) *extra virgin olive oil, plus extra for storing*

1 Put all of the ingredients, except the oil, into a food processor or blender and blitz together until fairly smooth.
2 With the motor running, gradually add enough oil to make a slightly sloppy mixture. Taste to check the seasoning.
3 Pour the pesto into sterilised jars, cover with a thin layer of oil and seal. This vibrant paste keeps for up to two weeks in the fridge.

FOR THE BASIL OIL:
PREPARATION: *10 minutes, plus standing*
MAKES: *600ml (1 pint)*

large handful basil leaves and stalks, lightly bruised
600ml (1 pint) *olive oil*

1 Put the ingredients into a large bowl or jar, making sure that the herbs are submerged. Cover and leave to infuse in a cool, dark place for two weeks to a month.
2 Strain the oil into sterilised bottles, seal and label. This oil keeps for six months in a cool, dark place.

FOR THE TAPENADE:
PREPARATION: *15 minutes*
MAKES: *about 300g (10½oz)*

1 *large clove garlic, chopped*
250g (9oz) *pitted black olives*
4 tbsp *capers, drained and rinsed*
8 *anchovy fillets, roughly chopped*
finely grated zest of 1 lemon
2–3 tbsp *extra virgin olive oil*

1 Whizz all of the ingredients, except the oil, in a food processor to make a coarse paste. Stir in enough olive oil to loosen.
2 Transfer into sterilised jars, seal and label. This savoury paste keeps for a month in the fridge.

Cute marshmallows and cinnamon-stick stirrers make this foodie kit much more than the sum of its parts.

HOT CHOCOLATE KIT

PREPARATION: *20 minutes*
MAKES: *6 sachets*

40g (1½oz) cocoa powder
85g (3oz) caster sugar
50g (1¾oz) dark chocolate drops

TO COMPLETE THE GIFT:
mini marshmallows
cinnamon sticks

A perfect gift for when the nights draw in and the fire goes on – friends and family will thank you from the bottom of their slippersocks.

1 Mix together the cocoa and sugar until well combined. Stir in the chocolate drops. Divide between six sachets (3 tsp in each) and seal.
2 To complete the gift, tuck a few sachets of the hot chocolate mix into a mug of your choosing along with a jar of mini marshmallows and a few cinnamon sticks tied with a ribbon. Write the instructions on a tag.
To make a mug of hot chocolate: Tip the contents of one sachet into your mug. Heat 200ml (7fl oz) of milk until piping hot, whisking often, then pour into the mug and stir with a cinnamon stick. Top with marshmallows and a spoonful of whipped cream, if you like.

SPICE BOX

FOR THE GARAM MASALA:

PREPARATION:
  10 minutes

MAKES: **9 teaspoons**

4 tbsp cardamom pods (or 1 tbsp cardamom seeds)
1 cinnamon stick, broken into pieces
2 tbsp coriander seeds
4 tsp black peppercorns
2 tsp whole cloves

Remove the seeds from the cardamom and discard the pods. Grind all the spices to a powder in an electric coffee grinder, a spice mill or a pestle and mortar. This mild blend for creamy curries keeps for up to two months.

FOR THE CHINESE FIVE SPICE:

PREPARATION:
  10 minutes

MAKES: **13 teaspoons**

12 star anise
2 tbsp Sichuan pepper
2 tbsp fennel seeds
4 tsp whole cloves
1 cinnamon stick, broken into pieces

Grind all the spices to a powder in an electric coffee grinder, a spice mill or a pestle and mortar. This mix is great for seasoning meat and poultry or in stir-fries and keeps for up to two months.

FOR THE ZA'ATAR:

PREPARATION:
  10 minutes

COOKING: **3 minutes**

MAKES: **17 teaspoons**

50g (1¾oz) sesame seeds
25g (1oz) sumac
10g (¼oz) dried thyme

Dry roast the sesame seeds in a small pan for a few minutes over a medium-low heat until they smell nutty. Cool, then mix with the sumac and thyme until thoroughly combined. Stir into yogurt for a dip or sprinkle on kebabs before cooking. This spice mix keeps for two months.

FOR THE MIXED SPICE:

PREPARATION:
  10 minutes

MAKES: **14 teaspoons**

1 cinnamon stick, broken into pieces
2 tbsp whole allspice
2 tbsp coriander seeds
4 tsp whole cloves
4 blades of mace
2 tsp ground ginger
4 tsp grated nutmeg

Grind all the spices to a powder in an electric coffee grinder, a spice mill or a pestle and mortar. This is a wonderful spice for baking and keeps for up to two months.

**FOR THE CAJUN
SEASONING:**
PREPARATION:
  10 minutes
MAKES: **10 teaspoons**

5 tsp hot paprika

1 tsp ground black pepper

2 tsp each cayenne pepper and ground
  cumin

1 tsp dried oregano

1 tsp dried thyme

Mix together all the ingredients until thoroughly combined. This seasoning is great to rub on fish, meat or poultry before grilling and keeps for up to two months.

A pleasing gift for novices or keen cooks who love to experiment with new flavours.

CONTAINERS AND PACKAGING

The fun for me doesn't stop with creating the food gifts themselves. I always keep an eye out for unusual wrappings and trimmings. I store these in a large box that I love to rummage through when the food is ready to package. The contents range from the mundane but indispensable items, such as waxed and greased paper and cellophane for lining tins and boxes, to the flourishes of ribbons, string, ink stamps, buttons and tags.

Don't forget an interesting container can be part of the gift, too: once eaten, a beautiful jar that contained chutney can be used for kitchen storage while a pretty tin emptied of biscuits or chocolates becomes a keepsake box to admire.

Vintage fairs, charity shops and antique centres are rich hunting grounds for unusual packaging. Usually cheap to buy, they'll be a unique way of presenting a gift and can be tailored to the recipient's taste or interests. Be inventive: a pretty cup and saucer can be filled with sweets while a cake can be presented on a beautiful antique stand. Whatever you choose, have fun!

GINGERBREAD HOUSE TEMPLATES

Use the measurements below to make your own templates for the pieces of gingerbread.

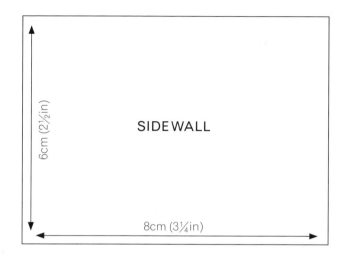

SIDE WALL

6cm (2½in)

8cm (3¼in)

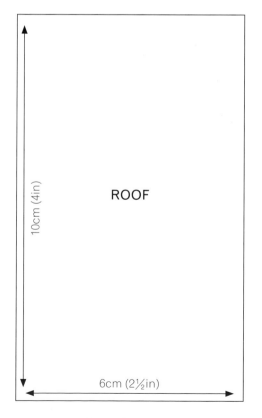

ROOF

10cm (4in)

6cm (2½in)

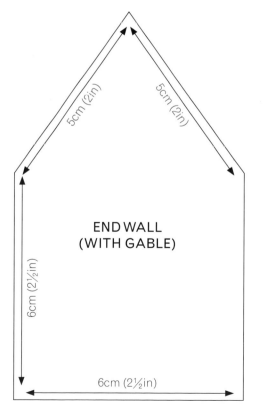

5cm (2in)

5cm (2in)

END WALL
(WITH GABLE)

6cm (2½in)

6cm (2½in)

STOCKISTS

COX AND COX
Paper, ribbons, tags
www.coxandcox.co.uk
0844 858 0744

WILLOW AND STONE
Paper, stickers, tapes, unusual
paper clips, coloured string, labels
and tags, ribbon, rubber stamps
www.willowandstone.co.uk
01326 311388

BAKERY BITS
Baking tins, trays and cases; paper
baking cases
www.bakerybits.co.uk
01404 565656

LAKELAND
Baking equipment, baking
cases, preserving equipment,
decorations, flavourings,
waxed paper
www.lakeland.co.uk
01539 488100

WARES OF KNUTSFORD
Preserving equipment and labels
www.waresofknutsford.co.uk
08456 121273

JAM JAR SHOP
Preserving equipment
www.jamjarshop.com
01572 720720

HOBBYCRAFT
Haberdashery, baking equipment,
art supplies
www.hobbycraft.co.uk
0330 026 1400

V V ROULEAUX
Ribbons
www.vvrouleaux.com
020 7224 5179

LIBERTY
Haberdashery, baking equipment,
patterned paper
www.liberty.co.uk
020 7734 1234

JOHN LEWIS
Haberdashery, baking equipment,
preserving equipment, cellophane
www.johnlewis.com
08456 049 049

PAPERCHASE
Stationery, paper, art materials
www.paperchase.co.uk

STEENBERGS
Spices and flavourings
www.steenbergs.co.uk
01765 640088

SEASONED PIONEERS
Spices and flavourings
www.seasonedpioneers.co.uk
0800 0682348

STAR KAY FLAVOURINGS
(such as peppermint, rose,
lavender, cinnamon, anise, lemon)
are available from Lakeland.

CRAFT COMPANY
Cake decorations, icing, food
pastes, cake cases, cookie cutters
www.craftcompany.co.uk
01926 888507

SQUIRES KITCHEN
Cake decorations, icing, food
pastes, cake cases, cookie cutters
www.squires-shop.com
0845 61 71 810

JANE ASHER
www.janeasher.com
020 7584 6177

CAKES, COOKIES AND CRAFTS
Cake decorations, icing, cake
cases, cookie cutters www.
cakescookiesandcraftsshop.co.uk
01524 389684

Most large supermarkets also
stock a good range of cake
decorations, cake cases and ready
made icings, food colourings and
flavourings.

Local post offices sell brown
paper, cellophane and plain
luggage tags.

INDEX

ACKNOWLEDGEMENTS

I would like to thank the following people for their help with this book:

Tara Fisher for her stunning photography and **Caroline Reeves** for the creative and beautiful propping. You are both a joy to work with.

The team at Jacqui Small: **Penny Stock, Jo Copestick** and, particularly, **Nikki Sims**, a brilliant and thorough editor who always asks the right questions.

The team at *Country Living* magazine – for being my official recipe tasters.

Most of all, my husband, **Keith**, for patiently ignoring and never complaining about the stacks of chutneys, pickles and jams, and tins of biscuits, sweets and cakes that took over our kitchen for more than six months… Thank you.

The publisher would also like to thank **Caroline Arber** for the photographs on the following pages: 28, 44–45, 59, 114–115, 118–119, 126, 135, 158–159; all other photographs by **Tara Fisher**.

Handmade Gifts
FROM THE KITCHEN